Economics
Rules

The Globalization Paradox:
Democracy and the Future of the World Economy

One Economics, Many Recipes:
Globalization, Institutions, and Economic Growth

Has Globalization Gone Too Far?

Economics Rules

THE RIGHTS AND WRONGS OF THE DISMAL SCIENCE

Dani Rodrik

W. W. NORTON & COMPANY
Independent Publishers Since 1923
New York | London

Manufacturing by RR Donnelley Harrisonburg
Book design by Chris Welch Design
Production manager: Julia Druskin

ISBN: 978-0-393-24641-4

W. W. Norton & Company, Inc.
500 Fifth Avenue, New York, N.Y. 10110
www.wwnorton.com

W. W. Norton & Company Ltd.
Castle House, 75/76 Wells Street, London W1T 3QT

1 2 3 4 5 6 7 8 9 0

CONTENTS

PREFACE AND

ACKNOWLEDGMENTS

This book has its origins in a course I taught with Roberto Mangabeira Unger on political economy for several years at Harvard. In his inimitable fashion, Roberto pushed me to think hard about the strengths and weaknesses of economics and to articulate what I found useful in the economic method. The discipline had become sterile and stale, Roberto argued, because economics had given up on grand social theorizing in the style of Adam Smith and Karl Marx. I pointed out, in turn, that the strength of economics lay precisely in small-scale theorizing, the kind of contextual thinking that clarifies cause and effect and sheds light—even if partial—on social reality. A modest science practiced with humility, I argued, is more likely to be useful than a search for universal theories about how capitalist systems function or what determines wealth and poverty around the world. I don't think I ever convinced him, but I hope he will find that his arguments did have some impact.

The idea of airing these thoughts in the form of a book finally jelled at the Institute for Advanced Study (IAS), to which I moved in the summer of 2013 for two enjoyable years. I had spent the bulk of my academic career in multidisciplinary environments, and I considered myself well exposed to—if not well versed in—different traditions within the social sciences. But the institute was a mind-stretching experience of an entirely different order of magnitude. The institute's School of Social Science, my new home, was grounded in humanistic and interpretive approaches that stand in sharp contrast to the empiricist positivism of economics. In my encounters with many of the visitors to the school—drawn from anthropology, sociology, history, philosophy, and political science, alongside economics—I was struck by a strong undercurrent of suspicion toward economists. To them, economists either stated the obvious or greatly overreached by applying simple frameworks to complex social phenomena. I sometimes felt that the few economists around were treated as the idiots savants of social science: good with math and statistics, but not much use otherwise.

The irony was that I had seen this kind of attitude before—in reverse. Hang around a bunch of economists and see what they say about sociology or anthropology! To economists, other social scientists are soft, undisciplined, verbose, insufficiently empirical, or (alternatively) inadequately versed in the pitfalls of empirical analysis. Economists know how to think and get results, while others go around in circles. So perhaps I should have been ready for the suspicions going in the opposite direction.

One of the surprising consequences of my immersion in the disciplinary maelstrom of the institute was that it made me feel better as an economist. I have long been critical of my fellow economists for being narrow-minded, taking their models too literally, and paying inadequate attention to social processes. But I felt that many of the criticisms coming from outside the field missed the point. There was too much misinformation about what economists really do. And I couldn't help but think that some of the practices in the other social sciences could be improved with the kind of attention to analytic argumentation and evidence that is the bread and butter of economists.

Yet it was also clear that economists had none other than themselves to blame for this state of affairs. The problem is not just their sense of self-satisfaction and their often doctrinaire attachment to a particular way of looking at the world. It is also that economists do a bad job of presenting their science to others. A substantial part of this book is devoted to showing that economics encompasses a large and evolving variety of frameworks, with different interpretations of how the world works and diverse implications for public policy. Yet, what noneconomists typically hear from economics sounds like a single-minded paean to markets, rationality, and selfish behavior. Economists excel at contingent explanations of social life— accounts that are explicit about how markets (and government intervention therein) produce different consequences for efficiency, equity, and economic growth, depending on specific background conditions. Yet economists often come across as pronouncing universal economic laws that hold everywhere, regardless of context.

I felt there was a need for a book that would bridge this divide—one aimed at both economists and noneconomists. My message for economists is that they need a better story about the kind of science they practice. I will provide an alternative framing highlighting the useful work that goes on within economics, while making transparent the pitfalls to which the practitioners of the science are prone. My message for noneconomists is that many of the standard criticisms of economics lose their bite under this alternative account. There is much to criticize in economics, but there is also much to appreciate (and emulate).

The Institute for Advanced Study was the perfect environment for writing this book in more than one way. With its quiet woods, excellent meals, and incredible resources, the IAS is a true scholars' haven. Faculty colleagues Danielle Allen, Didier Fassin, Joan Scott, and Michael Walzer stimulated my thinking about economics and provided inspiration with their contrasting, but equally exacting, models of scholarship. My faculty assistant, Nancy Cotterman, gave me useful feedback on the manuscript on top of her amazingly efficient administrative support. I am grateful to the institute's leadership, especially its director, Robbert Dijkgraaf, for allowing me to be part of this extraordinary intellectual community.

Andrew Wylie's guidance and advice ensured that the manuscript would end up in the right hands—namely, W. W.

Norton. At Norton, Brendan Curry was a wonderful editor and Stephanie Hiebert meticulously copyedited the manuscript; they both improved the book in countless ways. Special thanks to Avinash Dixit, a scholar who exemplifies the virtues of economists that I discuss in this book, who provided detailed comment and suggestions. My friends and coauthors Sharun Mukand and Arvind Subramanian generously gave their time and helped shape the overall project with their ideas and contributions. Last but not least, my greatest debt, as always, is to my wife, Pınar Doğan, who gave me her love and support throughout, in addition to helping me clarify my argument and discussion of economics concepts.

Economics
Rules

The Use and Misuse of Economic Ideas

D elegates from forty-four nations met in the New Hampshire resort of Bretton Woods in July 1944 to construct the postwar international economic order. When they left three weeks later, they had designed the constitution of a global system that would last for more than three decades. The system was the brainchild of two economists: the towering English giant of the profession, John Maynard Keynes; and the US Treasury official Harry Dexter White.*

---

* Whether White was actually a Soviet spy has been an ongoing controversy. The case against White was made forcefully in Benn Steil's *The Battle of Bretton Woods: John Maynard Keynes, Harry Dexter White, and the Making of a New World Order* (Princeton, NJ: Princeton University Press, 2013). For the argument on the other side, see James M. Boughton, "Dirtying White: Why Does Benn Steil's History of Bretton Woods Distort the Ideas of Harry Dexter White?" *Nation*, June 24, 2013. Whatever the facts of the case, it is clear that the International Monetary Fund and the World Bank

Keynes and White differed on many matters, especially where issues of national interest were at stake, but they had in common a mental frame shaped by the experience of the interwar period. Their objective was to avoid the upheavals of the last years of the Gold Standard and of the Great Depression. They agreed that achieving this goal required fixed, but occasionally adjustable, exchange rates; liberalization of international trade but not capital flows; enlarged scope for national monetary and fiscal policies; and enhanced cooperation through two new international agencies, the International Monetary Fund and the International Bank for Reconstruction and Development (which came to be known as the World Bank).

Keynes and White's regime proved remarkably successful. It unleashed an era of unprecedented economic growth and stability for advanced market economies, as well as for scores of countries that would become newly independent. The system was eventually undermined in the 1970s by the growth of speculative capital flows, which Keynes had warned against. But it remained the standard for global institutional engineering. Through each successive upheaval of the world economy, the rallying cry of the reformers was "a new Bretton Woods!"

In 1952, a Columbia University economist named William Vickrey proposed a new pricing system for the New

---

served quite well the economic interests of the United States (as well as those of the rest of the Western world) in the decades following the end of the Second World War.

York City subway. He recommended that fares be increased at peak times and in sections with high traffic, and be lowered at other times and in other sections. This system of "congestion pricing" was nothing other than the application of economic supply-demand principles to public transport. Differential fares would give commuters with more-flexible hours the incentive to avoid peak travel times. They would allow passenger traffic to spread out over time, reducing the pressure on the system while enabling even larger total passenger flow. Vickrey would later recommend a similar system for roads and auto traffic as well. But many thought his ideas were crazy and unworkable.

Singapore was the first country to put congestion pricing to a test. Beginning in 1975, Singaporean drivers were charged tolls for entering the central business district. This system was replaced in 1998 by an electronic toll, which made it possible to charge drivers varying rates depending on the average speed of traffic in the network. By all accounts, the system has reduced traffic congestion, increased public-transport use, reduced carbon emissions, and generated considerable revenue for the Singaporean authorities to boot. Its success has led other major cities, like London, Milan, and Stockholm, to emulate it with various modifications.

In 1997, Santiago Levy, an economics professor at Boston University serving as deputy minister of finance in his native Mexico, sought to overhaul the government's antipoverty approach. Existing programs provided assistance to the poor mainly in the form of food subsidies. Levy argued that these programs were ineffective and inefficient. A central tenet of economics holds that when it comes to the welfare of the poor, direct cash grants are more effective than subsidies on specific consumer goods. In addition, Levy thought he could use cash grants as leverage to improve outcomes on health and education. Mothers would be given cash; in return, they would have to ensure that their children were in school and receiving health care. In economists' lingo, the program gave mothers an incentive to invest in their children.

Progresa (later renamed *Oportunidades*, and later still, *Prospera*) was the first major conditional cash transfer (CCT) program established in a developing country. With the program scheduled for a gradual introduction, Levy also drew up an ingenious implementation scheme that would permit a clearcut evaluation of whether it worked, or not. It was all based on simple principles of economics, but it revolutionized the way policy makers thought about antipoverty programs. As the positive results came in, the program became a template for other nations. More than a dozen Latin American countries, including Brazil and Chile, would eventually adopt similar programs. A pilot CCT program was even instituted in New York City under Mayor Michael Bloomberg.

Three sets of economic ideas in three different areas: the world economy, urban transport, and the fight against poverty. In each case, economists remade part of our world by applying simple economic frameworks to public problems. These examples represent economics at its best. There are many others: Game theory has been used to set up auctions of airwaves for telecommunications; market design models have helped the medical profession assign residents to hospitals; industrial organization models underpin competition and antitrust policies; and recent developments in macroeconomic theory have led to the widespread adoption of inflation targeting policies by central banks around the world.[1] When economists get it right, the world gets better.

Yet economists often fail, as many examples in this book will illustrate. I wrote this book to try to explain why economics sometimes gets it right and sometimes doesn't. "Models"— the abstract, typically mathematical frameworks that economists use to make sense of the world—form the heart of the book. Models are both economics' strength and its Achilles' heel; they are also what make economics a science—not a science like quantum physics or molecular biology, but a science nonetheless.

Rather than a single, specific model, economics encompasses a collection of models. The discipline advances by expanding its library of models and by improving the mapping between these models and the real world. The diversity of models in economics is the necessary counterpart to the flexibility of the social world. Different social settings require different models. Economists are unlikely ever to uncover universal, general-purpose models.

But, in part because economists take the natural sciences as their example, they have a tendency to misuse their models.

They are prone to mistake a model for *the* model, relevant and applicable under all conditions. Economists must overcome this temptation. They have to select their models carefully as circumstances change, or as they turn their gaze from one setting to another. They need to learn how to shift among different models more fluidly.

This book both celebrates and critiques economics. I defend the core of the discipline—the role that economic models play in creating knowledge—but criticize the manner in which economists often practice their craft and (mis)use their models. The arguments I present are not the "party view." I suspect many economists will disagree with my take on the discipline, especially with my views on the kind of science that economics is.

In my interactions with many noneconomists and practitioners of other social sciences, I have often been baffled by outsider views on economics. Many of the complaints are well known: economics is simplistic and insular; it makes universal claims that ignore the role of culture, history, and other background conditions; it reifies the market; it is full of implicit value judgments; and besides, it fails to explain and predict developments in the economy. Each of these criticisms derives in large part from a failure to recognize that economics is, in fact, a collection of diverse models that do not have a particular ideological bent or lead to a unique conclusion. Of course, to the extent that economists themselves fail to reflect this diversity within their profession, the fault lies with them.

Another clarification at the outset. The term "economics" has come to be used in two different ways. One definition focuses on the substantive domain of study; in this interpretation, economics is a social science devoted to understanding how the economy works. The second definition focuses on methods: economics is a way of doing social science, using particular tools. In this interpretation the discipline is associated with an apparatus of formal modeling and statistical analysis rather than particular hypotheses or theories about the economy. Therefore, economic methods can be applied to many other areas besides the economy—everything from decisions within the family to questions about political institutions.

I use the term "economics" largely in the second sense. Everything I will say about the advantages and misapplication of models applies equally well to research in political science, sociology, or law that uses a similar approach. There has been a tendency in public discussion to associate these methods exclusively with a *Freakonomics* kind of work. This approach, popularized by the economist Steven Levitt, has been used to shed light on diverse social phenomena, ranging from the practices of sumo wrestlers to cheating by public school teachers, using careful empirical analysis and incentive-based reasoning.[2] Some critics suggest that this line of work trivializes economics. It eschews the big questions of the field—when do markets work and fail, what makes economies grow, how can full employment and price stability be reconciled, and so on—in favor of mundane, everyday applications.

In this book I focus squarely on these bigger questions and how economic models help us answer them. We cannot look to economics for universal explanations or prescriptions that apply regardless of context. The possibilities of social life are too diverse to be squeezed into unique frameworks. But each economic model is like a partial map that illuminates a fragment of the terrain. Taken together, economists' models are our best cognitive guide to the endless hills and valleys that constitute social experience.

CHAPTER 1

What Models Do

The Swedish-born economist Axel Leijonhufvud published in 1973 a little article called "Life among the Econ." It was a delightful mock ethnography in which he described in great detail the prevailing practices, status relations, and taboos among economists. What defines the "Econ tribe," explained Leijonhufvud, is their obsession with what he called "modls"—a reference to the stylized mathematical models that are economists' tool of the trade. While of no apparent practical use, the more ornate and ceremonial the modl, the greater a person's status. The Econ's emphasis on modls, Leijonhufvud wrote, explains why they hold members of other tribes such as the "Sociogs" and "Polscis" in such low regard: those other tribes do not make modls.*

---

* Axel Leijonhufvud, "Life among the Econ," *Western Economic Journal* 11, no. 3 (September 1973): 327. Since this article was published, the use of

Leijonhufvud's words still ring true more than four decades later. Training in economics consists essentially of learning a sequence of models. Perhaps the most important determinant of the pecking order in the profession is the ability to develop new models, or use existing models in conjunction with new evidence, to shed light on some aspect of social reality. The most heated intellectual debates revolve around the relevance or applicability of this or that model. If you want to grievously wound an economist, say simply, "You don't have a model."

Models are a source of pride. Hang around economists and before long you will encounter the ubiquitous mug or T-shirt that says, "Economists do it with models." You will also get the sense that many among them would get rather more joy out of toying with those mathematical contraptions than hanging out with the runway prancers of the real world. (No sexism is intended here: my wife, also an economist, was once presented one of those mugs as a gift from her students at the end of a term.)

For critics, economists' reliance on models captures almost everything that is wrong with the profession: the reduction of the complexities of social life to a few simplistic relationships, the willingness to make patently untrue assumptions, the obsession with mathematical rigor over realism, the frequent jump from stylized abstraction to policy conclusions. They find it mind-boggling that economists move so quickly from equa-

---

models has become more common in other social sciences, especially in political science.

tions on the page to advocacy of, say, free trade or a tax policy of one kind or another. An alternative charge asserts that economics makes the mundane complex. Economic models dress up common sense in mathematical formalism. And among the harshest critics are economists who have chosen to part ways with the orthodoxy. The maverick economist Kenneth Boulding is supposed to have said, "Mathematics brought rigor to economics; unfortunately it also brought mortis." The Cambridge University economist Ha-Joon Chang says, "95 percent of economics is common sense—made to look difficult, with the use of jargons and mathematics."[1]

In truth, simple models of the type that economists construct are absolutely essential to understanding the workings of society. Their simplicity, formalism, and neglect of many facets of the real world are precisely what make them valuable. These are a feature, not a bug. What makes a model useful is that it captures an aspect of reality. What makes it indispensable, when used well, is that it captures *the most relevant aspect of reality in a given context*. Different contexts—different markets, social settings, countries, time periods, and so on—require different models. And this is where economists typically get into trouble. They often discard their profession's most valuable contribution—the multiplicity of models tailored to a variety of settings—in favor of the search for the one and only universal model. When models are selected judiciously, they are a source of illumination. When used dogmatically, they lead to hubris and errors in policy.

A Variety of Models

Economists build models to capture salient aspects of social interactions. Such interactions typically take place in markets for goods and services. Economists tend to have quite a broad understanding of what a market is. The buyers and sellers can be individuals, firms, or other collective entities. The goods and services in question can be almost anything, including things such as political office or status, for which no market price exists. Markets can be local, regional, national, or international; they can be organized physically, as in a bazaar, or virtually, as in long-distance commerce. Economists are traditionally preoccupied with how markets work: Do they use resources efficiently? Can they be improved, and if so, how? How are the gains from exchange distributed? Economists also use models, however, to shed light on the functioning of other institutions—schools, trade unions, governments.

But what are economic models? The easiest way to understand them is as simplifications designed to show how specific mechanisms work by isolating them from other, confounding effects. A model focuses on particular causes and seeks to show how they work their effects through the system. A modeler builds an artificial world that reveals certain types of connections among the parts of the whole—connections that might be hard to discern if you were looking at the real world in its welter of complexity. Models in economics are no different from physical models used by physicians or architects. A plastic model of the respiratory system that you might encounter in a physician's office focuses on the detail of the lungs, leaving out the rest of the human body. An architect might build one model to present the landscape around a house, and another one to display the layout of the interior of the home. Economists' models are similar, except that they are not physical constructs but operate symbolically, using words and mathematics.

The workhorse model of economics is the supply-demand model familiar to everyone who has ever taken an introductory economics course. It's the one with the cross made up of a downward-sloping demand curve and an upward-sloping supply curve, and prices and quantities on the axes.* The artificial world here is the one that economists call a "perfectly competitive market," with a large number of consumers and producers. All of them pursue their economic interests, and none have the capacity to affect the market price. The model leaves many things out: that people have other motives besides material ones, that rationality is often overshadowed by emotion or erroneous cognitive shortcuts, that some producers can

---

* The supply-demand diagrams, along with the cross, apparently made their first appearance in print in 1838, in a book by the French economist Antoine-Augustin Cournot. Cournot is better known today for his work on duopoly, and the cross is usually attributed to the popular 1890 textbook by Alfred Marshall. See Thomas M. Humphrey, "Marshallian Cross Diagrams and Their Uses before Alfred Marshall: The Origins of Supply and Demand Geometry," *Economic Review* (Federal Reserve Bank of Richmond), March/April 1992, 3–23.

behave monopolistically, and so on. But it does elucidate some simple workings of a real-life market economy.

Some of these are obvious. For example, a rise in production costs increases market prices and reduces quantities demanded and supplied. Or, when energy costs rise, utility bills increase and households find extra ways of saving on heating and electricity. But others are not. For example, whether a tax is imposed on the producers or consumers of a commodity—say, oil—has nothing to do with who ends up paying for it. The tax might be administered on oil companies, but it might be consumers who really pay for it through higher prices at the pump. Or the extra cost might be imposed on consumers in the form of a sales tax, but the oil companies might be forced to absorb it through lower prices. It all depends on the "price elasticities" of demand and supply. With the addition of a longish list of extra assumptions—on which, more later—this model also generates rather strong implications about how well markets work. In particular, a competitive market economy is efficient in the sense that it is impossible to improve one person's well-being without reducing somebody else's. (This is what economists call "Pareto efficiency.")

Consider now a very different model, called the "prisoners' dilemma." It has its origins in research by mathematicians, but it is a cornerstone of much contemporary work in economics. The way it is typically presented, two individuals face punishment if either of them makes a confession. Let's frame it as an economics problem. Assume that two competing firms must decide whether to have a big advertising budget. Advertising would allow one firm to steal some of the other's customers. But when they both advertise, the effects on customer demand cancel out. The firms end up having spent money needlessly.

We might expect that neither firm would choose to spend much on advertising, but the model shows that this logic is off base. When the firms make their choices independently and they care only about their own profits, each one has an incentive to advertise, regardless of what the other firm does:* When the other firm does not advertise, you can steal customers from it if you do advertise; when the other firm does advertise, you have to advertise to prevent loss of customers. So the two firms end up in a bad equilibrium in which both have to waste resources. This market, unlike the one described in the previous paragraph, is not at all efficient.

The obvious difference between the two models is that one describes a scenario with many, many market participants (the market for, say, oranges) while the other describes competition between two large firms (the interaction between airplane manufacturers Boeing and Airbus, perhaps). But it would be a mistake to think that this difference is the exclusive reason

---

* Strictly speaking, another assumption is also needed: the firms have no way of making credible promises to each other—that is, promises they will not have the incentive to renege on later. For example, each firm may want to promise to the other that it will not advertise. But these promises are not credible, because each firm has an interest in advertising, regardless of what the other firm does.

that one market is efficient and the other not. Other assumptions built in to each of the models play a part. Tweaking those other assumptions, often implicit, generates still other kinds of results.

Consider a third model that is agnostic on the number of market participants, but that has outcomes of a very different kind. Let's call this the coordination model. A firm (or firms; the number doesn't matter) is deciding whether to invest in shipbuilding. If it can produce at sufficiently large scale, it knows the venture will be profitable. But one key input is low-cost steel, and it must be produced nearby. The company's decision boils down to this: if there is a steel factory close by, invest in shipbuilding; otherwise, don't invest. Now consider the thinking of potential steel investors in the region. Assume that shipyards are the only potential customers of steel. Steel producers figure they'll make money if there's a shipyard to buy their steel, but not otherwise.

Now we have two possible outcomes—what economists call "multiple equilibria." There is a "good" outcome, in which both types of investments are made, and both the shipyard and the steelmakers end up profitable and happy. Equilibrium is reached. Then there is a "bad" outcome, in which neither type of investment is made. This second outcome also is an equilibrium because the decisions not to invest reinforce each other. If there is no shipyard, steelmakers won't invest, and if there is no steel, the shipyard won't be built. This result is largely unrelated to the number of potential market participants. It depends crucially instead on three other features: (1) there are economies of scale (in other words, profitable operation requires large scale); (2) steel factories and shipyards need each other; and (3) there are no alternative markets and sources of inputs (that can be provided through foreign trade, for example).

Three models, three different visions of how markets function (or don't). None of them is right or wrong. Each highlights an important mechanism that is (or could be) at work in real-world economies. Already we begin to see how selecting the "right" model, the one that best fits the setting, will be important. One conventional view of economists is that they are knee-jerk market fundamentalists: they think the answer to every problem is to let the market be free. Many economists may have that predisposition. But it is certainly not what economics teaches. The correct answer to almost any question in economics is: It depends. Different models, each equally respectable, provide different answers.

Models do more than warn us that results could go either way. They are useful because they tell us precisely *what* the likely outcomes depend on. Consider some important examples. Does the minimum wage lower or raise employment? The answer depends on whether individual employers behave competitively or not (that is, whether they can influence the going wage in their location).[2] Does capital flow into an emerging-market economy raise or lower economic growth? It depends on whether the country's growth is constrained by lack of investable funds or by poor profitability due, say, to high taxes.[3]

Does a reduction in the government's fiscal deficit hamper or stimulate economic activity? The answer depends on the state of credibility, monetary policy, and the currency regime.[4]

The answer to each question depends on some critical feature of the real-world context. Models highlight those features and show how they influence the outcome. In each case there is a standard model that produces a conventional answer: minimum wages reduce employment, capital flow increases growth, and fiscal cutbacks hamper economic activity. But these conclusions are true only to the extent that their *critical assumptions*—the features of the real world identified above—approximate reality. When they don't, we need to rely on models with different assumptions.

I will discuss critical assumptions and give more examples of economic models later. But first a couple of analogies about what models are and what they do.

Models as Fables

One way to think of economic models is as fables. These short stories often revolve around a few principal characters who live in an unnamed but generic place (a village, a forest) and whose behavior and interaction produce an outcome that serves as a lesson of sorts. The characters can be anthropomorphized animals or inanimate objects, as well as humans. A fable is simplicity itself: the context in which the story unfolds is sketched in sparse terms, and the behavior of the characters is driven by stylized motives such as greed or jealousy. A fable makes little effort to be realistic or to draw a complete picture of the life of its characters. It sacrifices realism and ambiguity for the clarity of its story line. Importantly, each fable has a transparent moral: honesty is best, he laughs best who laughs last, misery loves company, don't kick a man when he's down, and so on.

Economic models are similar. They are simple and are set in abstract environments. They make no claim to realism for many of their assumptions. While they seem to be populated by real people and firms, the behavior of the principal characters is drawn in highly stylized form. Inanimate objects ("random shocks," "exogenous parameters," "nature") often feature in the model and drive the action. The story line revolves around clear cause-and-effect, if-then relationships. And the moral— or policy implication, as economists call it—is typically quite transparent: free markets are efficient, opportunistic behavior in strategic interactions can leave everyone worse off, incentives matter, and so on.

Fables are short and to the point. They take no chance that their message will be lost. The story of the hare and the tortoise imprints on your conscious mind the importance of steady, if slow, progress. The story becomes an interpretive shortcut, to be applied in a variety of similar settings. Pairing economic models with fables may seem to denigrate their "scientific" status. But part of their appeal is that they work in exactly the same way. A student exposed to the competitive supply-demand framework is left with an enduring respect for the power of markets. Once you work through the prisoners' dilemma, you can never think of problems of cooperation in quite the same way. Even when the specific details of the models are forgotten, they remain templates for understanding and interpreting the world.

The analogy is not missed by the profession's best practitioners. In their self-reflective moments, they are ready to acknowledge that the abstract models they put to paper are essentially fables. As the distinguished economic theorist Ariel Rubinstein puts it, "The word 'model' sounds more scientific than 'fable' or 'fairy tale' [yet] I do not see much difference between them."[5] In the words of philosopher Allan Gibbard and economist Hal Varian, "[An economic] model always tells a story."[6] Nancy Cartwright, the philosopher of science, uses the term "fable" in relation to economic and physics models alike, though she thinks economic models are more like parables.[7] Unlike fables, in which the moral is clear, Cartwright says that economic models require lots of care and interpretation in drawing out the policy implication. This complexity is related to the fact that each model captures only a contextual truth, a conclusion that applies to a specific setting.

But here, too, fables offer a useful analogy. There are countless fables, and each provides a guide for action under a somewhat different set of circumstances. Taken together, they result in morals that often appear contradictory. Some fables extol the virtues of trust and cooperation, while others recommend self-reliance. Some praise prior preparation; others warn about the dangers of overplanning. Some say you should spend and enjoy the money you have; others say you should save for a rainy day. Having friends is good, but having too many friends is not so good. Each fable has a definite moral, but in totality, fables foster doubt and uncertainty.

So we need to use judgment when selecting the fable that applies to a particular situation. Economic models require the same discernment. We've already seen how different models produce different conclusions. Self-interested behavior can result in both efficiency (the perfectly competitive market model) and waste (the prisoners' dilemma model) depending on what we assume about background conditions. As with fables, good judgment is indispensable in selecting from the available menu of contending models. Luckily, evidence can provide some useful guidance for sifting across models, though the process remains more craft than science (see Chapter 3).

Models as Experiments

If the idea of models as fables does not appeal, you can think of them as lab experiments. This is perhaps a surprising analogy. If fables make models seem like simplistic fairy tales, the comparison to lab experiments risks dressing them up in excessively scientific garb. After all, in many cultures lab experiments constitute the height of scientific respectability. They are the means by which scientists in white coats arrive at the "truth" about how the world works and whether a particular hypothesis is true. Can economic models come even close?

Consider what a lab experiment really is. The lab is an artificial environment built to insulate the materials involved in the experiments from the environment of the real world. The researcher designs experimental conditions that seek to highlight a hypothesized causal chain, isolating the process from other potentially important influences. When, say, gravity exerts confounding effects, the researcher carries out the experiment in a vacuum. As the Finnish philosopher Uskali Mäki explains, the economics modeler in fact practices a similar method of insulation, isolation, and identification. The main difference is that the lab experiment purposely manipulates the physical environment to achieve the isolation needed to observe the causal effect, whereas a model does this by manipulating the assumptions that go into it.* Models build mental environments to test hypotheses.

---

* Uskali Mäki, "Models Are Experiments, Experiments Are Models," *Journal of Economic Methodology* 12, no. 2 (2005): 303–15. Note that isolating an effect in economic models is not as simple as it may seem. We always have to make some assumptions about other background conditions. For this reason, Nancy Cartwright argues that the effect is always the result of the joint operation of many causes and we can never truly isolate cause and effect in economics. See Cartwright, *Hunting Causes and Using Them: Approaches in Philosophy and Economics* (Cambridge: Cambridge University Press, 2007). This is true in general, but the value of having multiple models is that it enables us to alter the background conditions selectively, to ascertain which, if any, make a substantive contribution to the effect.

You may object that in a lab experiment, as artificial as its environment may be, the action still takes place in the real world. We know if it works or does not work, in at least one setting. An economic model, by contrast, is a thoroughly artificial construct that unfolds in our minds only. Yet the difference can be in degree rather than in kind. Experimental results, too, may require significant extrapolation before they can be applied to the real world. Something that worked in the lab may not work outside it. For example, a drug might fail in practice when it mixes with real-world conditions that were left out of consideration—"controlled for"—under the experimental setting.

This is the distinction that philosophers of science refer to as internal versus external validity. A well-designed experiment that successfully traces out cause and effect in a specific setting is said to have a high degree of "internal validity." But its "external validity" depends on whether its conclusion can travel successfully outside the experimental context to other settings.

So-called field experiments, carried out not in the lab but under real-world conditions, also face this challenge. Such experiments have become very popular in economics recently, and they are sometimes thought to generate knowledge that is

---

Varying some background conditions may make a big difference; varying others, very little. See also my discussion on the realism of assumptions later in the chapter.

model-free; that is, they're supposed to provide insight about how the world works without the baggage of assumptions and hypothesized causal chains that comes with models. But this is not quite right. To give one example: In Colombia, the randomized distribution of private-school vouchers has significantly improved educational attainment. But this is no guarantee that similar programs would have the same outcome in the United States or in South Africa. The ultimate outcome relies on a host of factors that vary from country to country. Income levels and preferences of parents, the quality gap between private and public schools, the incentives that drive schoolteachers and administrators—all of these factors, and many other potentially important considerations, come into play.[8] Getting from "it worked there" to "it will work here" requires many additional steps.[9]

The gulf between real experiments carried out in the lab (or in the field) and the thought experiments we call "models" is less than we might have thought. Both kinds of exercises need some extrapolation before they can be applied when and where we need them. Sound extrapolation in turn requires a combination of good judgment, evidence from other sources, and structured reasoning. The power of all these types of experiments is that they teach us something about the world outside the context in which they're carried out, on account of our ability to discern similarity and draw parallels across diverse settings.

As with real experiments, the value of models resides in being able to isolate and identify specific causal mechanisms, one at a time. That these mechanisms operate in the real world alongside many others that may obfuscate their workings is a complication faced by all who attempt scientific explanations. Economic models may even have an advantage here. Contingency— dependence on specific postulated conditions—is built into them. As we'll see in Chapter 3, this lack of certainty encourages us to figure out which among multiple contending models provides a better description of the immediate reality.

Unrealistic Assumptions

Consumers are hyperrational, they are selfish, they always prefer more consumption to less, and they have a long time horizon, stretching into infinity. Economic models are typically assembled out of many such unrealistic assumptions. To be sure, many models are more realistic in one or more of these dimensions. But even in these more layered guises, other unrealistic assumptions can creep in somewhere else. Simplification and abstraction necessarily require that many elements remain counterfactual in the sense that they violate reality. What is the best way to think about this lack of realism?

Milton Friedman, one of the twentieth century's greatest economists, provided an answer in 1953 that deeply influenced the profession.[10] Friedman went beyond arguing that unrealistic assumptions were a necessary part of theorizing. He claimed that the realism of assumptions was simply irrelevant. Whether a theory made the correct predictions was all that mattered. As long as it did, the assumptions that went into the theory need not bear any resemblance to real life. While this is a crude summary of a more sophisticated argument, it does convey the gist that most readers took from Friedman's essay. As such, it was a wonderfully liberating argument, giving economists license to develop all kinds of models built on assumptions wildly at variance with actual experience.

However, it cannot be true that the realism of assumptions is entirely irrelevant. As Stanford economist Paul Pfleiderer explains, we always need to apply a "realism filter" to *critical* assumptions before a model can be treated as useful.[11] (Here's that term "critical" again. I will turn to it shortly.) The reason is that we can never be sure of a model's predictive success. Prediction, as Groucho Marx might have said, always involves the future. We can concoct an almost endless variety of models to explain a reality after the fact. But most of these models are unhelpful; they will fail to make the correct prediction in the future, when conditions change.

Suppose I have data on traffic accidents in a locality for the last five years. I notice that there are more accidents at the end of the workday, between 5:00 and 7:00 p.m. The most reasonable explanation is that more people are on the road at that time, driving home from work. But suppose a researcher comes up with an alternative story. It's John's fault, he says. John's brain emits invisible waves that affect everyone's driving. Once he is out of his office and on the street, his brain waves mess with traffic, causing more accidents. It may be a silly theory, but it does "explain" the rise in traffic accidents at the end of the workday.

We know in this case that the second model is not a useful one. If John changes his schedule or he retires, it will have no predictive value. The number of accidents will not go down when John is no longer out and about. The explanation fails because its critical assumption—that John emits traffic-disrupting brain waves—is false. For a model to be useful in the sense of tracking reality, its critical assumptions also have to track reality sufficiently closely.[12]

What exactly is a critical assumption? We can say an assumption is critical if its modification in an arguably more realistic direction would produce a substantive difference in the conclusion produced by the model. Many, if not most, assumptions are not critical in this sense. Consider the perfectly competitive market model. The answers to many questions of interest do not depend crucially on the details of that model. In his essay on methodology, Milton Friedman discussed taxes on cigarettes. We can safely predict that raising the tax rate will lead to an increase in the retail price of cigarettes, he wrote, regardless of whether there are many or few firms and whether different cigarette brands are perfect substitutes or not. Similarly, any reasonable relaxation of the requirement of perfect rationality would be unlikely to make much difference to that result. Even if firms do not make calculations to the last decimal point, we can be reasonably confident that they will notice an increase in

27

the taxes they have to pay. These specific assumptions are not critical in view of which question is posed and how the model is used—for example, how does a tax effect the price of cigarettes? Their lack of realism therefore is not of great importance.

Suppose we were interested in a different question: the effect of imposing price controls on the cigarette industry. Now the degree of competition in the industry, which depends in part on the extent to which consumers are willing to substitute between different brands, becomes of great importance. In the perfectly competitive market model, a price control leads to firms reducing their supply. The lower price decreases their profitability, and they respond by cutting back their sales. But in a model of a market that is monopolized by a single firm, a moderate price ceiling (that is, a ceiling that is not too far below the unrestricted market price) actually induces the firm to *increase* its output. To see how this mechanism operates, a bit of simple algebra or geometry comes in handy. Intuitively, a monopolist increases profits by restricting sales and raising the market price. Price controls, which rob the monopolist of its price-setting powers, effectively blunt the incentive to under-produce. The monopolist responds by increasing sales.* Selling more cigarettes is now the only means to making more profits.

What we assume about the degree of market competition becomes critical when we want to predict the effects of price

---

* This is the same logic that causes an increase in employment after a (moderate) minimum wage has been imposed.

controls. The realism of this particular assumption matters, and it matters greatly. The applicability of a model depends on how closely critical assumptions approximate the real world. And what makes an assumption critical depends in part on what the model is used for. I will return to this issue later in the book, when I examine in greater detail how we select which model to apply in a given setting.

It is perfectly legitimate, and indeed necessary, to question a model's efficacy when its critical assumptions are patently counterfactual, as with John's brain waves. In such instances, we can rightly say that the modeler has oversimplified and is leading us astray. The appropriate response, however, is to construct alternative models with more fitting assumptions—not to abandon models per se. The antidote to a bad model is a good model.

Ultimately, we cannot avoid unrealism in assumptions. As Cartwright says, "Criticizing economic models for using unrealistic assumptions is like criticizing Galileo's rolling ball experiments for using a plane honed to be as frictionless as possible."[13] But just as we would not want to apply Galileo's law of acceleration to a marble dropped into a jar of honey, this is not an excuse for using models whose critical assumptions grossly violate reality.

On Math and Models

Economic models consist of clearly stated assumptions and behavioral mechanisms. As such, they lend themselves to the language of mathematics. Flip the pages of any academic journal in economics and you will encounter a nearly endless stream of equations and Greek symbols. By the standards of the physical sciences, the math that economists use is not very advanced: the rudiments of multivariate calculus and optimization are typically sufficient to follow most economic theorizing. Nevertheless, the mathematical formalism does require some investment on the part of the reader. It raises a comprehensibility barrier between economics and most other social sciences. It also heightens noneconomists' suspicions about the profession: the math makes it seem as if economists have withdrawn from the real world and live in abstractions of their own construction.

When I was a young college student, I knew I wanted to get a PhD because I loved writing and doing research. But I was interested in a wide variety of social phenomena and could not make up my mind between political science and economics. I applied to both kinds of doctoral programs, but I postponed the ultimate decision by enrolling in a multidisciplinary master's program. I remember well the experience that finally resolved my indecision. I was in the library of the Woodrow Wilson School at Princeton and picked up the latest issues of the *American Economic Review* (*AER*) and the *American Political Science Review* (*APSR*), the flagship publications of the two disciplines. Looking at them side by side, it dawned on me that I would be able to read the *APSR* with a PhD in economics, but much of the *AER* would be inaccessible to me with a PhD in political science. With hindsight, I realize this conclusion was perhaps not quite right. The political philosophy articles in the *APSR* can be as abstruse as any in the *AER*, math aside. And much of political science has since gone the way of economics in adopting mathematical formalism. Nonetheless, there was a germ of truth in my observation. To this day, economics is by and large the only social science that remains almost entirely impenetrable to those who have not undertaken the requisite apprenticeship in graduate school.

The reason economists use mathematics is typically misunderstood. It has little to do with sophistication, complexity, or a claim to higher truth. Math essentially plays two roles in economics, neither of which is cause for glory: clarity and consistency. First, math ensures that the elements of a model— the assumptions, behavioral mechanisms, and main results— are stated clearly and are transparent. Once a model is stated in mathematical form, what it says or does is obvious to all who can read it. This clarity is of great value and is not adequately appreciated. We still have endless debates today about what Karl Marx, John Maynard Keynes, or Joseph Schumpeter really meant. Even though all three are giants of the economics profession, they formulated their models largely (but not exclusively) in verbal form. By contrast, no ink has ever been spilled over what Paul Samuelson, Joe Stiglitz, or Ken Arrow had in mind when they developed the theories that won them their Nobel. Mathematical models require that all the *t*'s be crossed and the *i*'s be dotted.

The second virtue of mathematics is that it ensures the internal consistency of a model—simply put, that the conclusions follow from the assumptions. This is a mundane but indispensable contribution. Some arguments are simple enough that they can be self-evident. Others require greater care, especially in light of cognitive biases that draw us toward results we want to see. Sometimes a result can be plainly wrong. More often, the argument turns out to be poorly specified, with critical assumptions left out. Here, math provides a useful check. Alfred Marshall, the towering economist of the pre-Keynesian era and author of the first real economics textbook, had a good rule: use math as a shorthand language, translate into English, and then burn the math! Or as I tell my students, economists use math not because they're smart, but because they're not smart enough.

When I was still young and green as an economist, I once heard a lecture by the great development economist Sir W. Arthur Lewis, winner of the 1979 Nobel Prize in Economic Sciences. Lewis had an uncanny ability to distill complex economic relationships to their essence by using simple models. But as with many economists from an older tradition, he tended to present his argument in verbal rather than mathematical form. On this occasion his topic was the determination of poor countries' terms of trade—the relative price of their exports to their imports. When Lewis finished, one of the younger, more mathematically oriented economists in the audience stood up and scribbled a few equations on the blackboard. He pointed out that at first he had been confused by what Professor Lewis was saying. But, he continued as a bemused Lewis watched, now he could see how it worked: we have these three equations that determine these three unknowns.

So, math plays a purely instrumental role in economic models. In principle, models do not require math, and it is not the math that makes the models useful or scientific.* As the Arthur Lewis example illustrates, some stellar practitioners of the craft rarely use any math at all. Tom Schelling, who has developed some of the key concepts of contemporary game theory, such as credibility, commitment, and deterrence, won the Nobel Prize for his largely math-free work.[14] Schelling has the rare knack of laying out what are fairly complicated models of interaction among strategically minded individuals while using only words, real-world examples, and perhaps a figure at most. His writings have greatly influenced both academics and policy makers. I must admit, though, that the depth of his insights and the precise nature of the arguments became fully evident to me only after I saw them expressed more fully with mathematics.

Nonmathematical models are more common in social sciences outside of economics. You can always tell that a social

---

* Outside of economics, the term "rational choice" has become a synonym for an approach to social science that uses predominantly mathematical models. This use of the term conflates several things. Doing social science using models requires neither math nor, necessarily, the assumption that individuals are rational.

scientist is about to embark on a model when he or she begins, "Assume that we have . . ." or something similar, followed by an abstraction. Here, for example, is the sociologist Diego Gambetta examining the consequences of different types of beliefs about the nature of knowledge: "Imagine two ideal-type societies that differ in one respect only . . ."[15] Papers in political science are frequently peppered with references to independent and dependent variables—a sure sign that the author is mimicking models even when a clear-cut framework is lacking.

Verbal arguments that seem intuitive often collapse, or are revealed to be incomplete, under closer mathematical scrutiny. The reason is that "verbal models" can ignore nonobvious but potentially significant interactions. For example, many empirical studies have found that government intervention is negatively correlated with performance: industries that receive subsidies experience lower productivity growth than industries that don't. How do we interpret these findings? It is common, even among economists, to conclude that governments must be intervening for the wrong rather than right reasons, that they support weak industries in response to political lobbying. This may sound reasonable—too obvious even to require further analysis. Yet when we mathematically describe the behavior of a government that intervenes for the right reason—by subsidizing industries to enhance the economy's efficiency—we see that this conclusion may not be warranted. Industries that are performing poorly because markets are malfunctioning warrant greater government intervention—

but not to the extent that their disadvantages are completely offset. Therefore, the negative correlation between subsidies and performance does not tell us whether governments are intervening in desirable or undesirable ways, as both types of intervention would generate the observed correlation. Not clear? Well, you can check the math!*

At the other end of the spectrum, too many economists fall in love with the math and forget its instrumental nature. Excessive formalization—math for its own sake—is rampant in the discipline. Some branches of economics, such as mathematical economics, have come to look more like applied mathematics than like any kind of social science. Their reference point has become other mathematical models instead of the

---

* Dani Rodrik, "Why We Learn Nothing from Regressing Economic Growth on Policies," *Seoul Journal of Economics* 25, no. 2 (Summer 2012): 137–51. Further afield from economics, John Maynard Smith, a distinguished theorist of evolutionary biology, explains why it is important to develop the mathematics of an argument in this video: http://www.webofstories.com/play/john.maynard.smith/52;jsessionid=3636304FA6745B8E5D200253DAF409E0. Maynard describes his frustration with a verbal theory of why some animals, like the antelope, jump up and down while running, exhibiting a behavior that is called "stotting." This behavior seems inefficient because it slows the animal down. The theory is that stotting is a way of signaling potential predators that the antelope is not worth pursuing: the antelope is so fast that it can get away even with this inefficient run. Smith recollects how he tried to model this scenario mathematically and could never produce the desired result—that stotting could be efficient when used as a signal.

real world. The abstract of one paper in the field opens with this sentence: "We establish new characterizations of Walrasian expectations equilibria based on the veto mechanism in the framework of differential information economies with a complete finite measure space of agents."[16] One of the profession's leading, and most mathematically oriented, journals (*Econometrica*) imposed a moratorium at one point on "social choice" theory—abstract models of voting mechanisms—because papers in the field had become mathematically so esoteric and divorced from actual politics.[17]

Before we judge such work too harshly, it is worth noting that some of the most useful applications in economics have come out of highly mathematical, and what to outsiders would surely seem abstruse, models. The theory of auctions, drawing on abstract game theory, is virtually impenetrable even to many economists.* Yet it produced the principles used by the Federal Communications Commission to allocate the nation's telecommunications spectrum to phone companies and broadcasters as efficiently as possible, while raising more than $60 billion for the federal government.[18] Models of matching and market design, equally mathematical, are used today to assign residents to hospitals and students to public schools. In each

---

* For a relatively informal introduction to the theory, see Paul Milgrom, "Auctions and Bidding: A Primer," *Journal of Economic Perspectives* 3, no. 3 (Summer 1989), 3–22. A more thorough treatment can be found in Paul Klemperer, *Auctions: Theory and Practice* (Princeton, NJ: Princeton University Press, 2004).

case, models that seemed to be highly abstract and to have few connections with the real world turned out to have useful applications many years later.

The good news is that, contrary to common perception, math for its own sake does not get you far in the economics profession. What's valued is "smarts": the ability to shed new light on an old topic, make an intractable problem soluble, or devise an ingenious new empirical approach to a substantive question. In fact, the emphasis on mathematical methods in economics is long past its peak. Today, models that are empirically oriented or policy relevant are greatly preferred in top journals over purely theoretical, mathematical exercises. The profession's stars and most heavily cited economists are those who have shed light on important public problems, such as poverty, public finance, economic growth, and financial crises—not its mathematical wizards.

Simplicity versus Complexity

Despite the math, economic models tend to be simple. For the most part, they can be solved using pen and paper. It's one reason why they have to leave out many aspects of the real world. But as we've seen, lack of realism is not a good criticism on its own. To use an example from Milton Friedman again, a model that included the eye color of the businesspeople competing against each other would be more realistic, but it would not be a better one.[19] Still, whether some influences matter or not depends on what is assumed at the outset. Perhaps blue-eyed businessmen are more dim-witted and systematically underprice their products. The strategic simplifications of the modeler, made for reasons of tractability, can have important implications for substantive outcomes.

Wouldn't it be better to opt for complexity over simplicity? Two related developments in recent years have made this question more pertinent. First, the stupendous increase in computing power and the attendant sharp fall in its cost have made it easier to run large-scale computational models. These are models with thousands of equations, containing nonlinearities and complex interactions. Computers can solve them, even if the human brain cannot. Climate models are a well-known example. Large-scale computational models are not unknown in economics, even though they are rarely as big. Most central banks use multiequation models to forecast the economy and predict the effects of monetary and fiscal policy.

The second development is the arrival of "big data," and the evolution of statistical and computational techniques that distill patterns and regularities from them. "Big data" refers to the humongous amount of quantitative information that is generated by our use of the Internet and social media—an almost complete and continuous record of where we are and what we do, moment by moment. Perhaps we have reached, or soon will reach, the stage where we can rely on the patterns revealed in this data to uncover the mysteries of our social relations. "Big data gives us a chance to view society in all its complexity," writes one of the leading proponents of this view.[20] This would send our traditional economic models the way of the horse and buggy.

Certainly, complexity has great surface appeal. Who could possibly deny that society and the economy are complex systems? "Nobody really agrees on what makes a complex system 'complex,'" writes Duncan Watts, a mathematician and sociologist, "but it's generally accepted that complexity arises out of many interdependent components interacting in nonlinear ways." Interestingly, the immediate example that Watts deploys is the economy: "The U.S. economy, for example, is the product of the individual actions of millions of people, as well as hundreds of thousands of firms, thousands of government agencies, and countless other external and internal factors, ranging from the weather in Texas to interest rates in China."[21] As Watts notes, disturbances in one part of the economy—say, in mortgage finance—can be amplified and produce major shocks for the entire economy, as in the "butterfly effect" from chaos theory.

It is interesting that Watts would point to the economy, since efforts to construct large-scale economic models have been singularly unproductive to date. To put it even more strongly, I cannot think of an important economic insight that has come out of such models. In fact, they have often led us astray. Overconfidence in the prevailing macroeconomic orthodoxy of the day resulted in the construction of several large-scale simulation models of the US economy in the 1960s and 1970s built on Keynesian foundations. These models performed rather badly in the stagflationary environment of the late 1970s and 1980s. They were subsequently jettisoned in favor of "new classical" approaches with rational expectations and price flexibility. Instead of relying on such models, it would have been far better to carry several small models in our heads simultaneously, of both Keynesian and new classical varieties, and know when to switch from one to the other.

Without these smaller, more transparent models, large-scale computational models are, in fact, unintelligible. I mean this in two senses. First, the assumptions and behavioral relations that are built into the large models must come from somewhere. Depending on whether you believe in the Keynesian model or the new classical model, you will develop a different large-scale model. If you think economic relationships are highly nonlinear or exhibit discontinuities, you will build a different model than if you think they are linear and "smooth." These prior understandings do not derive from complexity itself; they must come from some first-level theorizing.

Second, and alternatively, suppose we can build large-scale models relatively theory-free, using big-data techniques based on observed empirical regularities such as consumer spending patterns. Such models can deliver predictions, like weather models do, but never knowledge on their own. For they are like a black box: we can see what is coming out, but not the operative mechanism inside. To eke out knowledge from these models, we need to figure out and scrutinize the underlying causal mechanisms that produce specific results. In effect, we need to construct a small-scale version of the larger model. Only then can we say that we understand what's going on. Moreover, when we evaluate the predictions of the complex model—it predicted this recession, but will it predict the next one?—our judgment will depend on the nature of these underlying causal mechanisms. If they are plausible and reasonable, by the same standards we apply to small-scale models, we may have reason for confidence. Not otherwise.

Consider the large-scale computational models that are common in the analysis of international trade agreements among nations. These agreements change import and export policies in hundreds of industries that are linked through markets for labor, capital, and other productive inputs. A change in one industry affects all the others, and vice versa. If we want to understand the economy-wide consequences of trade agreements, we need a model that tracks all these interactions. In principle, that is what the so-called computable general equilibrium (CGE) models do. They are constructed partly on the basis of the prevalent models of trade, and partly on ad hoc assumptions meant to replicate observed economic regularities (such as the share of national output that is traded internationally). When pundits in the media report, say, that the Transatlantic Trade and Investment Partnership (TTIP) between the United States and Europe will create so many billions of dollars of exports and income, they are citing results from these models.

Without doubt, models of this sort can provide a sense of the orders of magnitude involved in a decision. But ultimately, they are credible only to the extent that their results can be motivated and justified by much smaller, pen-and-paper models. Unless the underlying explanation is transparent and intuitive—unless there exists a simpler model that generates a similar result—complexity on its own buys us nothing other than perhaps a bit more detail.

What about some of the specific insights arising out of models that emphasize complexity, such as tipping points, complementarities, multiple equilibria, or path dependence? It is true that such "nonstandard" outcomes emphasized by complexity theorists stand in sharp contrast to the more linear, smooth behavior of economists' workhorse models. It is also certainly true that real-world outcomes are sometimes better described in those spikier ways. However, not only can these kinds of outcomes be generated in smaller, simpler models, but they actually originate in them. Tipping-point models, referring to a sudden change in aggregate behavior after a sufficient number of individuals make a switch, were first developed and applied to different social settings by Tom Schelling. His paradigmatic example, developed in the 1970s, was the collapse of mixed neighborhoods into complete segregation once a critical threshold of white flight is reached. The potential for multiple equilibria has long been known and studied by economists, often in the context of highly stylized models. I gave an example (our shipbuilder and the coordination game) at the beginning of the chapter. Path dependence is a feature of a large class of dynamic economic models. And so on.

A critic might argue that economists treat such models as exceptions to the "normal" cases covered by the workhorse competitive market model. And the critic would have a point. Economists tend to fixate too much on certain standard models at the expense of others. In some settings, a simple model can be, well, too simple. We may need more detail. The trick is to isolate just the interactions that are hypothesized to matter, but no more. As the preceding examples suggest, models can do this and still remain simple. One model is not always better than another. Remember: it is *a* model, not *the* model.

Simplicity, Realism, and Reality

In his exceptionally brief—one paragraph, to be exact—short story called "On Exactitude in Science," the Argentine novelist Jorge Luis Borges describes a mythical empire in the distant past in which cartographers took their craft very seriously and strived for perfection. In their quest to capture as much detail as possible, they drew ever-bigger maps. The map of a province expanded to the size of a city; a map of the empire occupied a whole province. In time, even this level of detail became insufficient and the cartographers' guild drew a map of the empire on a 1:1 scale the size of the empire itself. But future generations, less enamored by the art of cartography and more interested in help with navigation, would find no use for these maps. They discarded them and left them to rot in the desert.[22]

As Borges's story illustrates, the argument that models need to be made more complex to make them more useful gets it backward. Economic models are relevant and teach us about the world *because* they are simple. Relevance does not require complexity, and complexity may impede relevance. Simple models—in the plural—are indispensable. Models are never true; but there is truth in models.[23] We can understand the world only by simplifying it.

CHAPTER 2

The Science of Economic Modeling

M odels make economics a science. With this assertion, I do not have in mind sciences like physics or chemistry, which seek to uncover fundamental laws of nature. Economics is a *social* science, and society does not have fundamental laws—at least, not in quite the same way that nature does. Unlike a rock or a planet, humans have agency; they choose what they do. Their actions produce a near infinite variety of possibilities. At best, we can talk in terms of tendencies, context-specific regularities, and likely consequences. Nor do I have in mind something like mathematics, which generates precise statements, albeit about abstract entities, that can be determined to be either true or false. Economics deals with the real world and is much messier than that. Economists often go astray precisely because they fancy themselves as physicists and mathematicians manqué.

At the other end of the spectrum, critics scoff at economists' scientific pretensions—chiding them for practicing make-believe science at best. Keynes, uncharacteristically, had a modest ambition for economics: "If economists could manage to get themselves thought of as humble, competent people, on a level with dentists, that would be splendid!" he wrote in 1930.[1] Perhaps even dentistry is too lofty a goal, in view of the variety of maladies and syndromes that afflict human societies. A good deal of modesty is in order about not only how much economists know, but also how much they can learn.

With those caveats out of the way, we can review what makes models scientific. First, as I explained in the previous chapter, models clarify the nature of hypotheses, making clear their logic and what they do and don't depend on. This is typically a matter of refining intuition, crossing the t's and dotting the i's—which is important in itself. But quite often their greater contribution is to open our eyes to counterintuitive possibilities and unexpected consequences. Second, models enable the accumulation of knowledge, by expanding the set of plausible explanations for, and our understanding of, a variety of social phenomena. In this way, economic science advances as a library would expand: by adding to its collection. Third, models imply an empirical method; they suggest how specific hypotheses and explanations can be applied, in principle at least, to actual settings. They enable arguments to be judged right or wrong. And even when evidence is too weak to discriminate among them, models provide a method for sorting out disagreements. Finally, models allow knowledge to be generated on the basis of commonly shared professional standards rather than prevailing hierarchies based on rank, personal connections, or ideology. The status of an economist's work depends, by and large, on its quality, not on his or her identity.

Clarifying Hypotheses

The grandiosely titled First Fundamental Theorem of Welfare Economics is probably the crown jewel of economics. (We will meet a close competitor shortly.) First-year doctoral students typically spend their first semester building up to a proof of this theorem, picking up a fair bit of mathematics (real analysis and topology) along the way that most will never use again. The theorem is nothing more than a mathematical statement of a key implication of what the previous chapter called the "perfectly competitive market model." It says, in brief, that a competitive market economy is efficient. More precisely, under the stated assumptions of the theorem, the market economy delivers as much economic output as any economic system possibly could. There is no way to improve on this outcome, in the sense that no reshuffling of resources could possibly leave someone better off without making some others worse off.* Note that this definition of efficiency—Pareto efficiency, named after the Italian polymath Vilfredo Pareto—pays no attention to equity or other possible social values: a market outcome in which one person receives 99 percent of total income would be "efficient" as long as his losses from any reshuffle exceeded the gains that would accrue to the rest of society.

Distributional complications aside, this is a powerful result—one that is not obvious. If today we associate markets readily with efficiency, it is largely because of more than two centuries of—let's not beat around the bush—indoctrination about the benefits of markets and capitalism. It is not at all evident, on its face, that millions of consumers, workers, firms, savers, investors, banks, and speculators, each of them pursuing strictly their own personal advantage, would collectively arrive at anything other than economic chaos. Yet the model says the outcome is actually efficient.

The First Fundamental Theorem of Welfare Economics is colloquially known among economists as the Invisible Hand Theorem. It was Adam Smith, perhaps the father of economics, who first stated it in broad terms. Though he did not use

---

* The Second Fundamental Theorem of Welfare Economics, in turn, is a statement about how alternative efficient outcomes can be reached via a suitable redistribution of resources, drawing, in essence, a distinction between questions of efficiency and distribution. More recent work has shown how this distinction crumbles when some of the premises of the two theorems—such as completeness of markets or information—fail to hold.

the term "invisible hand" in quite this context, Smith argued that decentralized decision making by individual consumers and producers in a market would nonetheless provide collective benefit. "It is not from the benevolence of the butcher, the brewer, or the baker, that we expect our dinner," he famously wrote, "but from their regard to their own interest."[2]

Smith's point that price incentives turn markets into a stupendously effective coordination machine running on autopilot was brought home powerfully by Milton Friedman in his popular TV series *Free to Choose* in 1980, on the eve of a wave of market reforms under the Reagan and Thatcher governments. Holding a pencil in his hand, Friedman marveled at the feat accomplished by free markets: it took thousands of people all over the world to make this pencil, he pointed out— to mine the graphite, cut the wood, assemble the components, and market the final product. Yet it was the price system, not any central authority, that managed to coordinate their actions so that the pencil would end up in the hands of the consumer.[3]

Compared to Adam Smith's and Milton Friedman's explications, the First Fundamental Theorem itself entails a logic that is highly abstract and almost impenetrably dense. It was first formulated fully in the early 1950s by Kenneth Arrow and Gerard Debreu, using mathematics that was then unfamiliar to most economists.[4] The first sentence of Debreu's 1951 article gives a sense of the nature of the exercise: "The activity of the economic system we study can be viewed as the transformation by n production units and the consumption by m consumption units of *l* commodities (the quantities of which may or may not be perfectly divisible)."* Even though the Arrow and Debreu articles are foundational, having earned each economist a Nobel Prize, they are rarely read. (I confess I looked at them for the first time as I was writing this.) Economists study them instead from textbooks and other secondhand treatments.

The First Fundamental Theorem is a big deal because it actually *proves* the Invisible Hand hypothesis. That is, it shows that under certain assumptions, the efficiency of a market economy is not just conjecture or possibility; it follows logically from the premises. The payoff from all the mathematics is that we actually have a precise statement. The model shows us exactly how the result is produced. It reveals, in particular, the specific assumptions that we have to make to be sure efficiency is achieved.

There is, in fact, a long list of such assumptions. Consumers and producers need to be rational and singularly focused on maximizing their economic advantage. We have to have markets in everything, including a full set of futures markets spanning all possible contingencies. Information has to be complete—meaning, for example, that consumers are knowledgeable about all attributes of a good even before purchasing and experiencing it. We need to rule out monopolistic behav-

---

* The joke is that when Debreu received the Nobel Prize in 1983, he was accosted by journalists who wanted to know his views about where the economy was headed. He is said to have thought awhile and then continued, "Imagine an economy with *n* goods and *m* consumers . . ."

ior on the part of producers, increasing returns to scale, and "externalities" (such as pollution or learning spillovers from R&D). Economists from Adam Smith on knew, of course, that such complications might interfere with the invisible hand. But Arrow and Debreu put it all together and made it all explicit and precise.

The First Fundamental Theorem is about a purely hypothetical world; it does not claim to describe any actual markets. Taking it to the real world requires judgment, evidence, and further theorizing. How one interprets its relevance for economic policy is a Rorschach test of sorts. For economic liberals and political conservatives, the theorem establishes the superiority of a market-based society. For the left, the long list of prerequisites demonstrates the virtual unattainability of efficiency through markets. The theorem on its own settles little in real-world policy debates. But no one could deny that, thanks to it and the literature it has spawned, we understand much better than we ever did the circumstances under which Adam Smith's Invisible Hand does and does not do its job.*

Let's turn now to another important example of how economic modeling helps clarify arguments that may be somewhat counterintuitive. In 1938, a young Paul Samuelson was chal-

---

* The assumptions needed to satisfy the Invisible Hand Theorem are *sufficient*, not necessary. In other words, markets can be efficient even when some of the assumptions fail. This bit of leeway enables some economists to argue that free markets are desirable even when the full Arrow-Debreu criteria are not met.

lenged by Stanislaw Ulam, the Polish-American mathematician, to state one proposition in the social sciences that is both true and nontrivial. Samuelson's answer was David Ricardo's Principle of Comparative Advantage. "Using four numbers, as if by magic, it shows that there is indeed a free lunch—a free lunch that comes with international trade."[5] Ricardo's demonstration, back in 1817, that specialization according to comparative advantage produces economic gains for all countries was as simple as it is powerful.[6] The nontrivial nature of the principle is obvious by how often it is misunderstood, even among sophisticated commentators. The antitrade sentiment attributed to Abraham Lincoln—"when we buy manufactured goods from abroad, we get the goods and the foreigner gets the money; when we buy the manufactured goods at home, we get the goods and we keep the money"—may be apocryphal, but not many can see easily through its illogic.

It was well understood long before Ricardo that cheap imports from other nations enabled a nation to economize on domestic resources such as labor and capital, which could then be put to alternative uses.[7] But how trade could possibly benefit both sides remained unclear. In particular, if a country was more efficient across the board, producing all goods while using fewer resources than other countries did, could it possibly gain from trade as well? Ricardo answered this question affirmatively. He laid out a numerical example, in what was one of the very first (and most successful) uses of models in economics. It was what economists call a 2×2 model of trade:

two countries (England and Portugal) and two commodities (cloth and wine).

Suppose, Ricardo wrote, it takes the labor of 80 workers to produce a given amount of wine in Portugal, and the labor of 90 workers to produce a given amount of cloth. In England, it takes 120 and 100 workers, respectively, to produce the same quantities of the two goods. Note that Portugal is more efficient than England in both cloth and wine. Nevertheless, Ricardo showed that Portugal would benefit by exporting wine to England and importing cloth in exchange. This way, Portugal could "obtain more cloth from England, than she could produce by diverting a portion of her capital from the cultivation of vines to the manufacture of cloth."[8] What generates the gains from trade is *comparative* advantage, not absolute advantage. A country benefits by exporting what it produces relatively less badly and importing what it produces relatively less well.

If this is not clear, remember what Samuelson said: the principle is not at all obvious. You do need to think and make a few calculations before it can sink in.

Ricardo's simple model clarified what the gains from trade did *not* depend on. A country did not have to be better than its trade partner at producing something to successfully export it. Neither did it have to be worse to benefit by importing it. Subsequent tinkering with the model by theorists over generations would clarify other things that the principle did not depend on. It did not matter how many commodities there were, or how many countries participated in trade; whether there were nontraded goods and services in addition to traded ones; whether trade was balanced in any given period; whether capital (or other resources) could move easily from one industry to another. It turns out none of these simplifications is critical, insofar as the Principle of Comparative Advantage and the gains from trade are concerned.

Further work would also clarify the principle's limitations. For example, some of the conditions under which the First Fundamental Theorem fails can also produce losses from trade. It is possible to come up with examples in which at least some countries lose out with trade in the presence of externalities or scale economies. Developing economies during the 1950s and 1960s became obsessed with this prospect and in response built up barriers against imports behind which they hoped their industries would flourish. And even when the gains from trade are there, they certainly do not imply that *everyone* in the nation will gain from trade. In fact, most extant models conclude that at least some groups end up worse off—employees of import-competing industries, or unskilled workers in a country that has a comparatively abundant number of skilled workers, for example. Someone who advocates free trade because it will benefit everyone probably does not understand how comparative advantage really works.

The Principle of Comparative Advantage and the First Fundamental Theorem of Welfare Economics are two of the clearest and most significant instances in which models have laid bare the nature of economic hypotheses—what they say exactly, why they work, and the conditions under which we can expect them to apply. But they are representative of a general style of inquiry. Is financial speculation good or bad for stability? Should we help poor families with cash grants or educational subsidies? Should monetary policy be discretionary or follow strict rules? The economists' approach in each case is to posit a model and check the conditions under which one or the other result prevails.

Direct evidence is rarely a substitute for disciplined thinking of this kind. Let's take an extreme case and suppose we're given evidence that decisively settles one of these questions. Such evidence will be necessarily specific to a particular geographic setting and time period: financial speculation did stabilize corn futures on the Chicago Board of Trade between 1995 and 2014, or direct cash grants were indeed more effective than subsidies for primary-school children in Tanzania between 2010 and 2012. As useful as evidence of this sort is, we need to embed it in economic models before we can interpret it appropriately. For example, were cash grants more effective than subsidies because of better incentives for families or because they reduced the workload of the bureaucrats administering the program? Extrapolating the evidence to other settings (or the future) also requires the use of models. Is financial speculation in, say, currency markets also stabilizing? Will speculation in corn futures still stabilize the market two years hence? Answering such questions requires models—

models that often remain vague and implicit. The more explicit the models are, the more transparent become the assumptions we're making to interpret and extrapolate evidence.

When Standard Intuition Fails Us

One of economists' many jokes about themselves is that "an economist is someone who sees something work in practice, and asks if it also works in theory." This might seem absurd, until we realize how easily intuition can lead us astray and how sometimes life delivers counterintuitive outcomes. Economic models can train our intuition to take in the possibility of such unexpected consequences. These surprises come under various guises.

The first category is "general-equilibrium interactions." To be distinguished from "partial-equilibrium" or single-market analysis, the term is a fancy way of saying we keep track of feedback effects across different markets. What happens in, say, labor markets affects goods markets, which in turn affects capital markets, and so on. Following this chain often seriously qualifies—and sometimes reverses—the conclusions of simple supply-demand models confined to one market at a time.

Consider immigration, a topic of great policy interest in the United States and other advanced economies. How does an increase in immigration—in, say, Florida—affect the labor market in the state? Our immediate intuition would be based on supply and demand: an increase in the supply of workers should reduce its price, wages. This impact of immigration would be pretty much the end of the story if there were no second- or third-round effects.

But what if local workers responded to the increased competition by moving out of state, to jobs in other parts of the country? What if the availability of a larger employee pool resulted in greater physical investment in the state, as firms moved in to build new factories and businesses? What if more workers at the low end of the skill distribution slowed down the introduction of new technologies? What if the migrant workers stimulated demand for the types of goods that are produced by migrant labor specifically? Each of these possibilities would tend to offset the initial impact of immigration. Something along these lines seems to have happened in 1980, when Miami received a large influx of Cuban immigrants—amounting to 7 percent of Miami's labor force—during the Mariel boatlift. UC Berkeley economist David Card found that the influx had virtually no effect on wages or unemployment in Miami, even among the least skilled workers, who were the most directly affected. While the precise reason for this outcome is still debated, it is likely that some combination of general-equilibrium effects was at work.[9]

Here's another example of how thinking in general-equilibrium terms is important. Suppose you are a highly skilled professional—an engineer, accountant, or experienced machinist—working in the US garment industry. Is expanded foreign trade with low-income countries like Vietnam or

Bangladesh good or bad for you? If you think only about what happens in the garment industry (that is, in partial-equilibrium terms), you'll conclude that you would be worse off. These countries likely will pose a severe competitive threat to US garment firms. But now consider the export side. As the wider US economy increases its exports to those new markets, which expand thanks to receipts from the United States, new employment opportunities arise in the growing export-oriented sectors. Since these expanding sectors are likely to be skill-intensive, they will want to hire lots of engineers, accountants, and experienced machinists. As these multimarket interactions work their way through the economy, you may find that your real compensation ends up higher than before, as demand increases for your skill set whether you move to another firm or not.[*]

Unexpected results also accrue from the economics of "second best." The General Theory of Second Best is among the most useful in the tool kit of applied economists, and perhaps the least intuitive to the untrained mind. It was first devel-

[*] This is the remarkable Stolper-Samuelson theorem, an extension of the basic Principle of Comparative Advantage. It says that opening up to trade benefits the factor of production that is relatively abundant (regardless of the sector where it is employed) and hurts the scarce factor. The crucial assumption it rests on is that different factors of production—workers of different skill types and capital—are mobile across industries. Wolfgang Stolper and Paul A. Samuelson, "Protection and Real Wages," *Review of Economic Studies* 9, no. 1 (1941): 58–73.

oped by James Meade in the context of trade policy, and subsequently generalized by Richard Lipsey and Kelvin Lancaster.[10] Its core insight observes that freeing up some markets, or opening a market that did not exist before, is not always beneficial when other, related markets remain restricted.

Early on, the theory was applied to trade agreements among a group of countries, such as the European Common Market. In these arrangements, participating countries free up trade among themselves, reducing or eliminating trade barriers vis-à-vis each other. The basic intuition from the Principle of Comparative Advantage suggests that all countries should reap the gains from trade. But that is not necessarily so. Thanks to the preferential nature of the barriers, France and Germany now trade more with each other, which is good. This phenomenon is known as the "trade creation effect." But for the same reason, Germany and France may now import even less from low-cost sources in Asia or the United States, which is bad. In the jargon, that's called the "trade diversion effect."

To see how trade diversion reduces economic well-being, imagine that beef is supplied by the United States to Germany at a price of $100. Assume that Germany imposes a tariff of 20 percent, raising the consumer price of US beef in the German market to $120. France, meanwhile, can supply beef of equivalent quality only at a price of $119. Prior to the preferential agreement between France and Germany, French suppliers, facing the same tariff rate as US producers, were outcompeted. Now consider what happens when Germany eliminates its tariffs on imports from France but keeps in place those on the United States. French-supplied beef suddenly becomes cheaper in Germany ($119 versus $120), and imports from the United States collapse. German consumers are better off by $1, but the German government forfeits $20 of tariff revenue previously collected on US beef (which could have been handed back to consumers or used to reduce other taxes in Germany). On balance, Germany gets a raw deal.

"Second best" logic applies to a wide variety of issues. One of the best known is Dutch disease syndrome, named after the consequences of the late-1950s discovery of natural gas in the Netherlands. Many observers subsequently noted that the competitiveness of Dutch manufacturing suffered in the 1960s, as the Dutch guilder strengthened in response to the gas bonanza and Dutch factories lost market share. The General Theory of Second Best clarifies the circumstances under which a resource boom can be (economically) bad news. The boom naturally crowds out some economic activities—such as manufacturing—because of the currency appreciation.* This in itself is not a problem: structural change is part and parcel of economic progress. But if the crowded activities were being underprovided in the first place—either because of government-imposed restrictions

---

* While currency appreciation is the more immediate mechanism, the same effect can be caused by an increase in domestic wages. Crowding out requires simply that domestic wages increase in foreign currency terms, which can happen because of a rise in wages, an increase in the value of the domestic currency, or some combination of the two.

or because they were the source of technological spillovers to other parts of the economy—then it is different. The economic losses from the contraction of important activities can even outweigh the direct gains from the resource boom. This is not of purely theoretical concern. Governments in resource-rich countries in sub-Saharan Africa face this challenge on a daily basis, as wage pressures emanating from lucrative mining activities erode their competitiveness in manufacturing.

Second-best interactions need not always reverse the standard conclusions; sometimes they strengthen the case for market liberalization. In the Dutch disease example, the adverse effect on manufacturing would be good news if the declining industries were "dirty" ones that caused environmental damages they did not pay for. But often the effect is to turn our standard intuitions upside down, with a move that appears to be in the right direction instead taking us further away from the target. Two wrongs can make a right. Since markets are never textbook perfect, such second-best problems pervade real life. As the Princeton economist Avinash Dixit says, "The world is second-best at best."[11] This means we have to be wary of economists' benchmark models, which presume well-functioning markets. Often they need to be tweaked by introducing some of the more salient market imperfections. Selecting the right model to apply is key.

Strategic behavior and interactions offer a third source of counterintuitive outcomes. We've already seen an example of this in the context of the prisoners' dilemma. Opportunistic behavior leads in this case to an outcome that each player would rather avoid. More broadly, as Thomas Schelling observed long ago, recognizing the presence of strategic interactions—what I do will affect what you do, and vice versa—can produce actions that would make little sense otherwise.[12] My threat to bomb you if you do not meet my demand is not credible as long as you retain the capacity to retaliate; so the threat is ineffective. But what if I act "crazy," sowing doubt in your mind that I am rational in the first place?

Strategic moves, designed to turn the interaction to one player's advantage, can take varied forms. To convince you that I will not negotiate my price down further before the deadline for reaching an agreement, I might simply cut off all communication—a strategy of "burning bridges." To prevent you from competing with me, I might build such excess capacity that, were you to enter my line of business, I would have the incentive to engage in aggressive price cutting that eventually would drive both of us into bankruptcy. To increase my trustworthiness as a borrower, I might contract with a third party (the mafia?) to impose a large cost on me (break my leg?) if I fail to pay back the money you lend to me.[13] In all these cases, actions that would not make sense outside the strategic context suddenly sound plausible in light of the intended goal of altering a competitor's or partner's cost-benefit calculus.

Finally, some counterintuitive outcomes arise out of the problem of "time-inconsistent preferences," which represent a conflict, loosely speaking, between what is desirable in the short run and what is desirable in the long run. Politicians may recognize that printing money only produces inflation in the long run, but they often cannot resist the temptation to inflate a little bit right now to stimulate some extra economic activity before they're up for election. Consumers know they should save for old age, but often they cannot stop maxing out their credit cards. These examples are a kind of strategic interaction, except that the interaction takes place between today's self and the future self. The inability of today's self to commit to the desirable pattern of behavior harms the future self.

The generic solution to these problems is a strategy of precommitment. In the inflation example, the policy maker might choose to delegate monetary policy to an independent central bank that is tasked with price stability alone or is run by an ultraconservative banker. In the saving example, someone might ask an employer to make automatic deductions to a retirement plan. The paradox in these cases is that reducing one's freedom of action can make one better off, defying the usual economic dictum that more choice is always better than less. But the paradox is only an illusion. What is a paradox for one class of models is often readily comprehensible within another class of models.

Scientific Progress, One Model at a Time

Ask an economist what makes economics a science, and the reply is likely to be, "It's a science because we work with the scientific method: we build hypotheses and then test them. When a theory fails the test, we discard it and either replace it or come up with an improved version. Ultimately, economics advances by developing theories that better explain the world."

This is a nice story, but it bears little relationship to what economists do in practice and how the field really makes progress.* For one thing, much of economists' work departs significantly from the hypothetico-deductive mold according to which hypotheses are first formulated and then confronted with real-world evidence. A more common strategy is to formulate models in response to a particular regularity or outcome that existing models don't appear to explain—for example, the apparently perverse behavior of banks to ration how much they lend to firms instead of charging them higher interest rates. The researcher develops a new model that he or she claims better accounts for the "deviant" observations.

In the case of credit rationing, default risk is a plausible explanation: raising interest rates above a certain threshold would lead the borrower to gamble on increasingly risky projects,

---

* Ever since Thomas Kuhn's *The Structure of Scientific Revolutions* (Chicago: University of Chicago Press, 1962), it has become commonplace to question whether even the natural sciences fit this idealized mold. Kuhn pointed out that scientists work within "paradigms" that they're unwilling to give up even in the presence of evidence that violates them. My point about economics will be different. It is that economics as a science advances "horizontally" (by multiplying models) rather than "vertically" (by newer ones replacing older ones).

since the losses are capped at the lower end. Thanks to limited liability, the borrower might not be forced to turn over to his creditors an amount greater than his marketable assets.[14] The resulting model might be presented as a deduction from first principles. That, after all, is the accepted view of economists' scientific method. But in fact, the thinking that produced the model involved a large element of induction. And since the model is specifically devised to account for a particular empirical reality, it can't be directly tested by being confronted with that same reality. In other words, credit rationing cannot itself constitute a test of the theory, since it's what motivated the theory in the first place.

Moreover, even when a truly deductive, hypothesis-testing approach is followed, much of what economists produce is not really testable in any strict sense of the word. The field is rife with models that yield contradictory conclusions, as we've seen. Yet very few of the models that economists work with have ever been rejected so decisively that the profession discarded them as clearly false. Considerable academic activity purports to provide empirical support for this or that model. But these exercises are typically brittle, their conclusions often weakened (or overturned) by subsequent empirical analysis. Consequently, the profession's progression of favored models tends to follow fad and fashion, or changing tastes about what is an appropriate modeling strategy, instead of evidence per se.

The sociology of the profession is a subject for a later chapter. The more fundamental point is that the fluidity of social reality makes economic models inherently difficult, even impossible, to test. First, the social world rarely delivers clean evidence that would allow a researcher to draw clear-cut inferences about the validity of alternative hypotheses. Most questions of interest—what makes economies grow? does fiscal policy stimulate the economy? do cash transfers reduce poverty?—cannot be studied in the laboratory. The causes we look for are typically confounded by a jumble of interactions in the data we have. Despite econometricians' best efforts, convincing causal evidence is notoriously elusive.

An even greater obstacle is that we cannot expect any of our economic models to be universally valid. One can debate whether there are many universal laws, even in physics.* But, as I have emphasized repeatedly, economics is something else.

---

* Here is the physicist Steven Weinberg: "None of the laws of physics known today (with the possible exception of the general principles of quantum mechanics) are exactly and universally valid. Nevertheless, many of them have settled down to a final form, valid in certain known circumstances. The equations of electricity and magnetism that are today known as Maxwell's equations are not the equations originally written down by Maxwell; they are equations that physicists settled on after decades of subsequent work by other physicists. . . . They are understood today to be an approximation that is valid in a limited context . . . but in this form and in this limited context they have survived for a century and may be expected to survive indefinitely. This is the sort of law of physics that I think corresponds to something as real as anything else we know." Weinberg, "Sokal's Hoax," *New York Review of Books* 43, no. 13 (August 8, 1996): 11–15.

In economics, context is all. What is true of one setting need not be true of another. Some markets are competitive; others, not. Some require second-best analysis; others may not. Some political systems face time-inconsistent problems in monetary policy; others don't. And so on. It is not surprising to find—as with, say, privatization of state assets or import liberalization—that the responses of different societies to quite similar policy interventions often vary greatly. Savvy economists end up applying different models to make sense of divergent outcomes. This reliance on multiple models does not reflect the inadequacy of our models; it reflects the contingency of social life.

Knowledge accumulates in economics not vertically, with better models replacing worse ones, but horizontally, with newer models explaining aspects of social outcomes that were unaddressed earlier. Fresh models don't really replace older ones. They bring in a new dimension that may be more relevant in some settings.

Consider how economists' understanding of the most basic question in economics has evolved: How do markets really work? In the beginning, the focus was markets that were fully competitive, with a large number of producers and consumers, none of whom could influence market prices. It was in the context of such competitive markets that the fundamental efficiency properties of a market economy were established. But there was also an early strand of work that analyzed outcomes when markets were imperfectly competitive, either monopolized by a single producer or dominated by a couple of large firms. It was well recognized that behavior in these markets differed profoundly from the competitive benchmark.

Unlike the competitive model, which comes essentially in unique form, the number and variety of imperfectly competitive models are limited only by the researcher's imagination. In addition to monopolies and duopolies, we have "monopolistic competition" (a large number of firms, each with market power in a different brand), Bertrand versus Cournot competition (different assumptions about how prices are set), static versus dynamic models (which affect the degree of collusion that can be sustained by firms), simultaneous versus sequential moves (which determine whether there might be first-mover advantages), and so on. Depending on what we assume along these and many other dimensions, we have learned from decades of modeling that imperfect competition can produce a bewildering array of possibilities. More important, thanks to the transparency of the assumptions, we have also learned what each one of these outcomes is predicated on.

In the 1970s, economists began to model another aspect of markets: asymmetric information. This is an important feature of real-world markets. Workers have a better sense of their ability than do employers. Creditors know whether they are likely to default or not, while lenders do not. Buyers of used cars do not know whether they're buying a lemon, but sellers do. Work by Michael Spence, Joseph Stiglitz, and George Akerlof showed that these types of markets could exhibit a variety of distinctive features, including signaling (costly investment in behavior that has no immediate apparent benefit), rationing (refusal to provide a good or service, even at a higher price), and market collapse. This work earned these three economists a joint Nobel Prize in 2001 and spawned a huge literature that hums along to this day. As a result, we understand much better the workings of credit and insurance markets, where information asymmetries are rife.*

Today, economists are increasingly turning their attention to markets in which consumers do not behave fully rationally.

---

* In his Nobel address, here's how George Akerlof described the shift in economic modeling of which he was part: "At the beginning of the 1960s, standard microeconomic theory was overwhelmingly based upon the perfectly competitive general equilibrium model. By the 1990s the study of this model was just one branch of economic theory. Then, standard papers in economic theory were in a very different style from now, where economic models are tailored to specific markets and specific situations. In this new style, economic theory is not just the exploration of deviations from the single model of perfect competition. Instead, in this new style, the economic model is customized to describe the salient features of reality that describe the special problem under consideration. Perfect competition is only one model among many, although itself an interesting special case. Since the 'Market for "Lemons"' [the research that won Akerlof his Nobel Prize] was an early paper in this new style of economics, its origins and history are a saga in that change." Akerlof, "Writing the 'The Market for "Lemons"': A Personal and Interpretive Essay" (2001 Nobel Prize lecture), http://www.nobelprize.org/nobel_prizes/economic-sciences/laureates/2001/akerlof-article.html?utm_source=facebook&utm_medium=social&utm_campaign=facebook_page.

This reorientation has produced a new field called behavioral economics, which attempts to integrate the insights of psychology with the formal modeling approaches of economics. These new frameworks hold great promise when consumers behave in ways that cannot be explained by extant models— when, for example, they walk half a mile to get to another store where a soccer ball sells for $2 less but would not do the same to save $100 on an expensive stereo. Many standard conclusions no longer apply when behavior is driven by norms or heuristics—rules of thumb—rather than cost-benefit considerations. The irrelevance of sunk costs (payments already made that cannot be recouped) and the equivalence between financial costs and opportunity costs (the value of choices not exercised) do not hold under less than full rationality, to cite but two examples.

Although grossly simplified, this telescopic account should give a sense of the expanding diversity of the profession's explanatory models. We have moved beyond competitive models to imperfect competition, asymmetric information, and behavioral economics. Idealized, flawless markets have given way to markets that can fail in all sorts of ways. Rational behavior is being overlaid with findings from psychology. Typically, the expansion has its roots in empirical observations that seem to contradict existing models. Why, for example, were many firms paying their workers wages that were substantially higher than the going market wage for apparently similar workers?[15] Why would more parents show up late to pick up their kids when the day care center began to charge them a fine for doing so?* Each question precipitated new models.

The newer generations of models do not render the older generations wrong or less relevant; they simply expand the range of the discipline's insights. The garden-variety perfectly competitive market model remains indispensable for answering many real-world questions. We do not have to be concerned with asymmetric information in a range of contexts—in repeated purchases of simple consumer goods, for example— because people tend to learn over time relevant characteristics such as quality and durability. And we would go badly wrong if we assumed consumer behavior is always driven by heuristics, with rationality rarely playing a role. Older models remain useful; we add to them.

Progress? Yes, definitely so. Economists' understanding of markets has never been as sophisticated as it is today. But it's a different kind of progress than in the natural sciences. Its horizontal expansion does not presume there are fixed laws of

* This is the famous Israeli day care center experiment reported in Uri Gneezy and Aldo Rustichini, "A Fine Is a Price," *Journal of Legal Studies* 29, no. 1 (January 2000): 1–17. The authors interpret the result as a consequence of modification of the information environment in which the parents make their decisions, in a way that is more or less compatible with the usual rationality postulates. An interpretation based on a shift in norms once the fine has been introduced is provided by Samuel Bowles, "Machiavelli's Mistake: Why Good Laws Are No Substitute for Good Citizens" (unpublished book manuscript, 2014).

nature waiting to be discovered. It seeks instead to uncover and understand society's possibilities.

Itzhak Gilboa and his coauthors provide a useful analogy in their distinction between rule-based and case-based learning.[16] "In everyday as well as professional life," they write, "people use both rule-based reasoning and case-based reasoning for making predictions, classifications, diagnostics, and for making ethical and legal judgments." Rule-based reasoning has the advantage that it provides a compact way of organizing a large volume of information, even though it may sacrifice some accuracy in particular applications. Case-based reasoning, on the other hand, works via analogies, drawing on other cases that present similarities. When the relevant data cannot be forced into succinct rules without sacrificing too much relevance, the case-based approach becomes particularly useful. As Gilboa and his coauthors note, "Some of the practices that evolved in economics can be better understood if scientific knowledge can also be viewed as a collection of cases." In this perspective, economic science advances by expanding its collection of useful cases.

Models and Empirical Methods

The multiplicity of models is economics' strength. But for a discipline with scientific pretensions, the multiplicity can also be viewed as problematic. What kind of a science has a different model for everything? Can a collection of cases, to use Gilboa and his coauthors' analogy, really amount to a science?

Yes, as long as we keep in mind that models contain information about the circumstances in which they're relevant and applicable. They tell us when we can use them, and when we might not. To continue the analogy, economic models are cases that come with explicit user's guides—teaching notes on how to apply them. That's because they are transparent about their critical assumptions and behavioral mechanisms.

This means that, in any specific setting, we can discriminate, at least in principle, between models that are helpful and models that aren't. Should we apply the competitive model or the monopoly model to, say, the PC industry? The answer depends on whether significant barriers—such as large sunk costs or anticompetitive practices—prevent potential competitors from entering the market. Should we worry about second-best complications like Dutch disease or trade diversion? The answer depends largely on whether specific market imperfections—technological spillovers from manufacturing and trade barriers against third countries, respectively—are present and important. Actually, a lot more goes into this process of navigating among models, as I'll discuss more extensively in the next chapter. But precisely because models lay bare how specific assumptions are needed to produce certain results, they can be sorted by context. The multiplicity of models does not imply that anything goes. It simply means we have a menu to choose from and need an empirical method for making that choice.

I do not want to claim that empirical verification necessarily or always works well. But even when the empirical data are inconclusive, models enable rational and constructive debate because they clarify sources of disagreement. In economics, policy discussion usually means pitting one model against another. Viewpoints and policy prescriptions that aren't backed by a model typically don't have standing. And once the models are produced, it becomes clear to all what each side assumes about the real world. This may not resolve the disagreement. Indeed, typically it doesn't, given the different ways that each side is likely to read reality. But at least we can expect that the two sides will eventually agree on what they disagree about.

These kinds of debates take place endlessly in economics. For example, the controversy over the effects of redistributive taxation largely boils down to the shape of the labor supply curve of entrepreneurs. Those who think that entrepreneurship does not respond much to income incentives are much less worried about raising taxes than are those who believe that entrepreneurship is highly sensitive to incentives. Probably the topics that provoke the fiercest debates in the profession are the roles of monetary and fiscal policy in a recession. These debates are essentially about whether recovery is hampered by the economy's demand curve or supply curve. If you believe aggregate demand is repressed, you will generally be in favor of monetary and fiscal stimulus. If you think the problem is supply shock—because of excessive taxation, say, or policy uncertainty—your remedies will be quite different. Occasionally, empirical evidence will accumulate to the point where the profession's preference for one set of models over another will become overwhelming. This is what happened, for example, in development economics, where the hypothesis of the ignorant peasant was discarded in the 1960s in favor of models of the calculating peasant, once it became clear that poor farmers' responsiveness to prices was much greater than many had thought.[*]

One debate I've been involved in focuses on the role of industrial policy in low- and middle-income countries.[17] These are government policies such as cheap credit or subsidies designed to foster structural change, from traditional low-productivity activities such as subsistence agriculture to modern, productive industries such as manufacturing. Critics have traditionally scoffed at them by calling them a strategy of "picking winners"—a fool's errand, in other words. Economic research has clarified over the years that the rationale for such policies is quite strong in the environment that characterizes developing economies. For a variety of reasons, related to both market and government failures, modern firms and industries would be smaller than they should be if left to market forces alone.

[*] Theodore W. Schultz, a Nobel Prize winner, led the way. Schultz, *Transforming Traditional Agriculture* (New Haven, CT: Yale University Press, 1964).

Research has also shown that governments have many ways of stimulating positive structural change without picking winners— by investing in a portfolio of new industries as venture capital firms do, for example. Above all, various models have clarified that the real debate is not about industrial policy and economics, but about the nature of government. If government can be a force for good and intervene effectively, at least occasionally, then some kind of industrial policy should be favored. If instead government is hopelessly corrupt, industrial policy will likely make things worse. Note how, in this case, research has pushed the disagreement onto a domain—public administration—in which economists have no particular expertise.

Models, Authority, and Hierarchy

Two well-known economists, Carmen Reinhart and Kenneth Rogoff, published a paper in 2010 that would become fodder in a political battle with high stakes.[18] The paper appeared to show that public-debt levels above 90 percent of GDP significantly impede economic growth. Conservative US politicians and European Union officials latched on to this work to justify their ongoing call for fiscal austerity. Even though Reinhart and Rogoff's interpretation of their results was considerably more cautious, the paper became exhibit A in the fiscal conservatives' case for reducing public spending despite the economic downturn.

A graduate student in economics at the University of Massachusetts at Amherst, Thomas Herndon, then did what academics are routinely supposed to do: replicate others' work and subject it to criticism. Along with a relatively minor spreadsheet error, he identified some methodological choices in the original Reinhart-Rogoff work that threw the robustness of their results into question. Most important, even though debt levels and growth remained negatively correlated, the evidence for a 90 percent threshold appeared weak. And, as many others also had argued, the correlation itself could be the result of low growth leading to high indebtedness, rather than the other way around. When Herndon published his critique, coauthored with UMass professors Michael Ash and Robert Pollin, it set off a firestorm.[19]

Because the 90 percent threshold had become politically charged, its subsequent demolition also gained broader political meaning. Reinhart and Rogoff vigorously contested accusations by many commentators that they were willing, if not willful, participants in a game of political deception. They defended their empirical methods and insisted that they were not the deficit hawks their critics portrayed them to be. Despite their protests, they were accused of providing scholarly cover for a set of policies for which there was, in fact, limited supporting evidence.

The controversy over the Reinhart-Rogoff analysis overshadowed what, in fact, was a salutary process of scrutiny and refinement of economic research. Reinhart and Rogoff quickly acknowledged the spreadsheet mistake they had made. The dueling analyses clarified the nature of the data, their limitations, and how alternative methods of processing changed the results. Ultimately, Reinhart and Rogoff were perhaps not that far apart from their critics on either what the evidence showed or what the policy implications were; they certainly did not believe in a rigid threshold of 90 percent, and they agreed that the correlation between high debt and low growth could have different interpretations. The episode's silver lining reveals that economics can progress by the rules of science. No matter how far apart their political views may have been, the two sides shared a common language about what constitutes evidence and—for the most part—a common approach to resolving differences.

The fracas was frequently portrayed in the media as two world-famous Harvard professors brought low by a graduate student from a lesser-known, unorthodox department. This is largely hyperbole. But the clash did illustrate an import aspect of economics—something that the profession shares with other sciences: Ultimately, what determines the standing of a piece of research is not the affiliation, status, or network of the author; it is how well it stacks up to the research criteria of the profession itself. The authority of the work derives from its internal properties—how well it is put together, how convincing the evidence is—not from the identity, connections, or ideology of the researcher. And because these standards are shared within the profession, anyone can point to shoddy work and say it is shoddy.*

This may not seem particularly impressive, unless you consider how unusual it is compared to many other social sciences or much of the humanities.† It would be truly rare in those other fields for a graduate student to get much mileage challenging a senior scholar's work, as happens with some frequency

---

* On the difference between social sciences whose standards of argumentation and evidence pass this test and those whose standards do not, see Jon Elster, *Explaining Social Behavior: More Nuts and Bolts for the Social Sciences* (Cambridge: Cambridge University Press, 2007), especially pp. 445–67. A very different interpretation of economics is provided in Marion Fourcade, Etienne Ollion, and Yann Algan, *The Superiority of Economists*, MaxPo Discussion Paper 14/3 (Paris: Max Planck Sciences Po Center on Coping with Instability in Market Societies, 2014). These authors interpret the consensus on the academic hierarchy within the discipline as a tight form of control exercised by the top departments in the discipline. The sharing of norms about what constitutes good work, as in many natural sciences, is an equally plausible explanation for this consensus.

† In a famous hoax, physicist Alan Sokal submitted an article to a leading journal of cultural studies purporting to describe how quantum gravity could produce a "liberatory postmodern science." The article, which parodied the convoluted style of argument in the fashionable academic world of cultural studies, was promptly published by the editors. Sokal announced that his intention was to test the intellectual standards of the discipline by checking whether the journal would publish a piece "liberally salted with nonsense." Sokal, "A Physicist Experiments with Cultural Studies," April 15, 1996, http://www.physics.nyu.edu/sokal/lingua_franca_v4.pdf.

in economics. But because models enable the highlighting of error, in economics anyone can do it.

There is a flip side to this apparent democracy of ideas that is less salutary. Because economists share a language and method, they are prone to disregard, or deprecate, noneconomists' points of view. Critics are not taken seriously—what is your model? where is the evidence?—unless they're willing to follow the rules of engagement. Only card-carrying members of the profession are viewed as legitimate participants in economic debates—hence the paradox that economics is highly sensitive to criticism from inside, but extremely insensitive to criticism from outside.

Wrong versus Not Even Wrong

The Swiss-Austrian physicist Wolfgang Pauli, a pioneer of quantum physics, was known for his high standards and cutting wit. As a young and unknown student, he once endorsed a comment made by Einstein in a colloquium by saying "You know, what Mr. Einstein said is not so stupid." Pauli was particularly critical of arguments that had scientific pretensions but were poorly stated and had no way of being tested. Upon being shown such a work by a younger physicist, his response was, "It's not even wrong."[20]

What Pauli probably meant is that it was impossible to challenge the work because no clear, coherent argument had been put forth. The assumptions, causal links, and implications were so vague as to render the supposed contribution irrefutable—under any circumstances. "It's not even wrong" is just about as damning a comment for scholarly effort as one might imagine. Having sat through quite a few talks that left me with precisely this sentiment, I can attest that it is not an irregular occurrence. My obvious bias aside—and apologies to my noneconomist colleagues—obscurity of this kind happens a lot less frequently in economics than in other disciplines.

The scientific status I have claimed for economics is not a particularly exalted one. It lies far from the positivist ideal, first articulated by the French philosopher Auguste Comte in the early part of the 19th century, whereby a combination of logic and evidence produces ever-higher degrees of certainty about the nature of social life.* Both the generality and the testability of economic propositions are limited. Economic science is merely disciplined intuition—intuition rendered transparent by logic and hardened by plausible evidence. "The whole of science," Einstein once said, "is nothing but a refinement of everyday thinking."[21] At their best, economists' models provide some of that refinement—and not much more.

---

* My take on economics is, in fact, much closer to the pragmatist tradition in epistemology than to the positivist one.

CHAPTER 3

Navigating among Models

W hat makes economics a science is models. It becomes a *useful* science when those models are deployed to enhance our understanding of how the world works and how it can be improved. Identifying which models to use means parsing and selecting—focusing on models that seem relevant and helpful to a specific setting, while discarding the rest. How this sifting is done in practice— or more important, how it should be done—is the subject of this chapter. But first a warning: these methods are as much craft as they are science. Good judgment and experience are indispensable, and training can get you only so far. Perhaps as a consequence, graduate programs in economics pay very little attention to craft.

Freshly minted PhDs come out of graduate school with a large inventory of models but virtually no formal training—no course work, no assignments, no problem sets—in how one chooses among them. The models they end up working with are typically the newest, the ones that have caught the profession's interest in the most recent generation of research. Graduates who eventually become good applied economists pick up the requisite skills along the way, as they are confronted with policy questions and challenges during their professional lives. But unfortunately, few able practitioners bother to systematize what they've learned, in the form of books or articles, for the benefit of less experienced members of the discipline.

Model selection also gets short shrift in economics in light of the profession's official take on what kind of science it is. As I've discussed already, the party line holds that economics advances by improving existing models and testing hypotheses. Models are continually refined until the true universal model comes into view. Hypotheses that fail the test are discarded; those that pass are retained. This way of thinking leaves little room for the idea that economists have to carry multiple models in their heads simultaneously, and that they must build maps between specific settings and applicable models.

If all that economists do is expand the library of models—if, in other words, they are pure theorists—they can't do much harm. But most economists are engaged also in more practical things. In particular, they are interested in two related questions: how does the world really work, and how can we improve on the state of things? To judge by the attention their work gets in public discussion, the world expects practical relevance of them too. Answering the second of these questions usually requires having an answer to the first. The positive and the normative analyses—investigations, respectively, of what is and what should be—are deeply intertwined. In economists' terms, both questions translate to this: What is the underlying model?

I have stressed that a model is never an accurate description of any reality. As David Colander and Roland Kupers put it, "Scientific models provide, at best, half-truths."[1] So when economists ask, "What is the underlying model?" they are not asking for the best possible representation of the market, region, or country they happen to be analyzing. Even if they could develop such a representation, it would be far too complicated and thus useless. They are asking for the model that highlights the *dominant causal mechanism or channels* at work. This model will provide the best explanation of what's happening and stands the best chance of predicting the consequences of our actions.

Imagine that your car has a problem and you want to figure out what's wrong and how to fix it. You could pick apart the entire car, piece by piece, in the hope of eventually encountering the broken part. This is not merely time-consuming, but may not even lead you to the solution. A car is a system, after all. The problem may reside in the way different components relate to each other—or fail to relate—instead of in specific components. Alternatively, you could try to diagnose first which of the car's many subsystems—brakes, transmission, and so on—led to the malfunction. Your diagnosis can draw from a wide variety of signals: what happened just before the car broke down, how the car responds as you turn the ignition on, and of course, the more thorough software-based diagnostics that today's repair shops routinely use. The exercise will eventually lead you to the culprit: perhaps the cooling or ignition system. Now you can focus only on the subsystem that needs fixing.

All parts of the car are required for it to run: transmission, cooling, ignition. So we can say they are all "causal" to the movement of the car. But the dominant mechanism in explaining the failure is only one of these. The rest are incidental to the question at hand. A more complicated and realistic model of the car—say, a full-size working replica, like Jorge Luis Borges's famous map the size of the world—wouldn't be of much help. What helps is knowing what to focus on. By the same token, the "correct" economic model is the one that isolates the critical relationships, allowing us to understand what is really causal among all the things going on. And the way we arrive at the right model is not very different from the kind of diagnostics we perform on a car.

Diagnostics for Growth Strategy

My own aha! moment about diagnostics came as I was assisting governments of developing nations with their economic programs. The countries varied greatly—from South Africa to El Salvador, from Uruguay to Ethiopia. But in each case my colleagues and I faced the same central question: what kinds of policies should the government adopt to increase the economy's growth rate and raise the incomes of all social strata, the disadvantaged groups in particular.

There was typically no shortage of proposals for reform.

- Some analysts would focus on skills, training, and improving the country's base of human capital.
- Some would focus on macroeconomic policy, recommending ways to strengthen monetary and fiscal policies.
- Some thought the country needed greater openness to trade and foreign investment.
- Some said taxes on private enterprise were too high and there were too many other costs of doing business.
- Some recommended industrial policies to restructure the economy and foster new, high-productivity industries.
- Some advised tackling corruption and strengthening property rights.
- Some came down in favor of infrastructure investments.

Until recently, multilateral institutions such as the World Bank usually would have thrown all these recommendations into a document and, voilà! we would have a growth strategy. By the 1990s, policy makers were forced to acknowledge that this process did not work very well. A laundry-list approach to developing policy presented governments with an impossibly ambitious agenda that they had no chance of implementing. Governments invariably failed to deliver on most of the intended reforms. And those they did follow through on were not necessarily the most important ones, so the economies' response remained tepid. Meanwhile, outside advisers would skirt blame by pointing to "slippages in reform" or "reform fatigue" on the part of their clients.[2]

My colleagues and I advocated a more strategic approach, prioritizing a narrower range of reforms. The reforms had to be targeted at the largest obstacles, avoiding the risk that governments would waste large amounts of political capital with little economic growth in return. But which reforms, among the long list above, fit the bill?

The answer depended on the favored model of growth. Those of us who looked at growth from the perspective of the "neoclassical model" emphasized the supply of physical and human capital and the barriers it faced. Those who preferred "endogenous" growth models, in which growth is driven by investment in new technologies, homed in on the environment for market competition and innovation. Those who had worked intensively with models that put institutional quality at center stage concentrated on property rights and contract enforcement. Those who were steeped in "dual economy" models would look at the conditions for structural transformation and the transition from traditional economic activities such as subsistence agriculture to modern firms and industries. Each one of these models provided a different entry point to the problem and emphasized a different set of priorities.

Once it became clear that our differences on policy were the result of favoring different models, the discussion became a lot clearer. Now we could understand where each one of us was coming from. More important, we could begin to narrow our differences by confronting the separate models informally with the evidence at hand. What should we be seeing if this or that model was true—that is, captured the most important mechanism behind growth in that particular setting? What kind of evidence would help us determine the more relevant of two models with different implications? Since we did not have the luxury of waiting for all the needed data to accumulate, or to carry out randomized or laboratory experiments on actual economies, we had to do this in real time, with the evidence at hand.

Eventually, we developed a decision tree that helped us navigate across potential models.[3] The tree looks something like the chart shown on the next page, which omits many of the details. We would start at the top of the tree by asking whether the constraints on investment were mainly on the supply side or on the demand side. In other words, was investment depressed because of inadequate supply of funds or poor returns? If the constraints were on the supply side, we would ask whether they were due mainly to a lack of saving or to a poorly functioning financial system. If they were on the demand side, we would ask whether private returns were low because of market or government failures. If the culprit seemed to be government failures, was this a matter of high taxes, corruption, or policy instability? And so on.

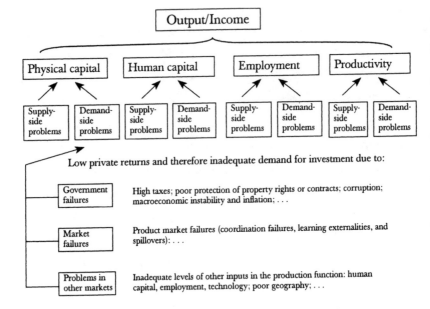

FROM GROWTH MODELS TO GROWTH DIAGNOSTICS.

Source: Dani Rodrik, "Diagnostics before Prescription," *Journal of Economic Perspectives* 24, no. 3 (Summer 2010): 33-44. Note: Only some of the details are shown.

At each node of the decision tree, we tried to develop informal empirical tests to help us select among models that would send us down different paths. For example, when the main problem of an economy is inadequate supply of capital, as in the neoclassical growth model, borrowing costs will be inversely related to investment. Reductions in the cost of capital will be associated with a strong investment response. Further, any increase in transfers from abroad, such as workers' remittances or foreign aid, will ignite a domestic investment boom. Sectors that are the most capital-intensive or most dependent on borrowing will be those that have the slowest growth. Did the implications of the model match up with observed behavior of the economy in question? If yes, the answer to "What is the underlying model?" might indeed be a version of the neoclassical growth model.

On the other hand, in an economy constrained by investment demand, private investment would respond primarily to profitability shocks in goods markets. When entrepreneurs are deterred by corruption, for example, their primary concern will be whether they can retain the returns on their investments. Availability of funds will not make much difference to their behavior. A surge in remittances or foreign capital inflow would produce a boom in consumption rather than investment. (This is the case shown in the chart.) These, too, are implications that could be checked against observed reality.[4]

Even though the available evidence rarely settled such questions once and for all, it was often possible to pare down a long catalog of failures to a considerably shorter list. In the case of South Africa, we were able to dismiss fairly quickly some of the conventional culprits that preoccupied policy makers: shortage of skills, poor governance, macroeconomic instability, bad infrastructure, or lack of openness to trade. The recent behavior of the economy did not support a conclusion that any of these were major constraints. The model-based approach forced us to think in economy-wide (that is, general-equilibrium) rather than partial-equilibrium terms. For example, business people would complain about the difficulty of finding skilled workers, which had led many observers to believe skill shortages were a major obstacle. But this conclusion was belied by the fact that the most rapidly expanding segments of the economy had been, in fact, the skill-intensive parts, such as finance. Whatever was holding back the economy as a whole could not have been lack of skills. The framework instead revealed a few critical problem areas—the high cost of unskilled labor and the lack of competitiveness of most manufacturing industries in particular.[5]

The virtue of diagnostic analysis is that it does not presume that a single model applies to all countries. When we worked on El Salvador, in Central America, we concluded that a model with market failures in modern industries provided a better account of the economy's woes. Low investment and growth could not be explained by inadequacy of funds, poor institutions and policies, low skills, high cost of labor, or other possible factors. For example, the Salvadoran economy received plenty of remittances from abroad and had good access to international capital markets, thanks to its credit rating. So the problems were not on the supply side of investment. Low investment seemed instead to be the product of difficulties that firms faced in getting started in the more modern, productive parts of the economy. Some of these difficulties arose from pervasive coordination failures, of the type I discussed in Chapter 1. For instance, pineapple canneries could not operate profitably without frequent air cargo service to the US market. But the cargo service was not profitable without a large number of existing exporters, such as pineapple canneries. Other problems included inadequate information on costs and markets in new lines of business, given the absence of pioneer firms whose experience could have otherwise provided valuable signals to aspiring entrants. Our policy recommendations correspondingly focused on these particular problem areas.[6]

Nor does the diagnostic approach presume that the underlying model remains the same over time for a given country. As circumstances change, a different model may become more relevant. In fact, if the initial diagnosis is largely correct and the government effectively addresses the problems, the underlying model, by necessity, will be transformed. For example, as market failures in modern manufacturing industries are overcome, infrastructure constraints (for example, ports, energy) may become much more severe. Or skill shortages may become the more dominant obstacle. Model selection is a dynamic process, not a onetime affair.

General Principles of Model Selection

Let's step back now from the specifics of growth diagnostics. Experience helps to highlight some general rules and practices. The key skill is being able to move back and forth between the candidate models and the real world. Let's call this "verification." The process of model selection relies on some combination of four separate verification strategies:

1. Verifying critical assumptions of a model to see how well they reflect the setting in question

2. Verifying that the mechanisms posited in the model are, in fact, operating

3. Verifying that the direct implications of the model are borne out

4. Verifying whether the incidental implications, those that the model generates as a by-product, are broadly consistent with observed outcomes

Verifying Critical Assumptions

As I've already discussed, what matters to the empirical relevance of a model is the realism of its *critical* assumptions. These assumptions would produce a substantively different result if they were altered to be more realistic. Many assumptions may be harmless in this sense. Others can be critical for some types of questions the model answers but not for others.

Consider a case in which a government concerned with the high price of oil is contemplating a price cap. Answering this question requires a view—a model—of how the market for oil works. Let's simplify things greatly and restrict our attention to two contending models: the competitive model and the monopoly model. Proponents of the competitive model see high prices as the result of too little supply relative to demand.

In this model a price cap—a ceiling above which oil companies cannot charge more—would not be particularly effective. It would create a gap between the amount of oil that consumers demanded and the amount that producers were willing to supply. There would be rationing, queues, or some other way of eliminating the gap. The market price of oil would, in fact, be likely to rise as total supply fell. Some people might get the oil at a cheaper price by being at the front of the queue or by being allotted rations, but others would surely pay the higher price. Not a very good policy overall.

Proponents of the monopoly model see high prices as the result of the oil industry acting as a cartel. In this model the industry would create an artificial shortage by withholding supplies from the market in order to engineer a price rise, thereby increasing the industry's profits. A price cap would produce very different results in this model. Once the cap was instituted, firms would no longer be able to determine market prices by changing how much they sold. They would now act as price-taking firms; in other words, they would behave in the same way that firms in the competitive model would.* If the price cap was not set too low, the total supply would rise and the market price would fall. The cartel would collapse, and the price cap would be effective because it acted as a trust-busting policy.

---

* I'm neglecting here some questions about the mechanism by which the cartel operates, and assuming simply that the cartel acts like a unified monopoly.

What are the critical and noncritical assumptions in these models' descriptions of the world? First, both models are about the supply side of the industry—how the oil firms behave. Therefore we can leave aside their assumptions about consumers and how they make their choices. Whether they are fully rational, possess full information, vary in their incomes and preferences, or have long time horizons is not of much interest. The only critical assumption on the demand side is that there is a downward-sloping market demand curve, meaning that an increase in the price of oil causes a reduction in the quantity of oil consumed, everything else remaining the same. This proposition is plausible under a very large range of circumstances and can be empirically verified. These other issues may become critical in some contexts—for example, when we're discussing the distributional effects of oil taxes—but they do not help us choose between the two contending models in this case. The second assumption is that strategic dimensions besides price-setting behavior do not play a role either. So we may also ignore implicit or explicit assumptions about, say, firms' hiring or advertising strategies.

The truly critical assumption here is that firms have market power in one case and not in the other. In the monopolistic model they think they can raise the market price by restricting supply, whereas in the competitive model they hold no such hope. In some ways, this is an assumption about firms' psychology. We cannot get into their managers' heads to figure out what they really believe. Asking them the question point-blank is not likely to yield a reliable answer, given their stake in the issue. But we can examine prevailing conditions to see whether a particular set of beliefs is more plausible.

The number and size distribution of firms in the industry will play an important role. If the number is large and there are no dominant firms, it is unlikely that firms will be able to or will act noncompetitively. How easily new firms can enter the industry is another important consideration. Even if few firms currently occupy the space, the threat of new competitors will deter them from exercising market power. Moreover, the oil industry is global rather than national. Competition from foreign producers can act as a source of market discipline at the margin, even when import volumes are small. Finally, the more easily consumers can substitute between oil and alternative sources of energy, the less likely it is that oil firms will be able to exert market power. Each one of these factors can be observed and measured in principle. Indeed, national antitrust authorities routinely perform this kind of a diagnostic exercise when they suspect that firms have (and are abusing) market power.

Models often make assumptions that are critical but unstated. Failing to scrutinize those assumptions can lead to severe problems in practice. Economists and policy makers learned this the hard way during the 1980s–90s frenzy over market liberalization. Freeing up prices and removing market restrictions, many thought, would be enough for markets to work and allocate resources efficiently. But all models of market economies presume the existence of various social, legal, and political institutions. Property rights and contracts must be enforced, fair competition must be ensured, theft and extortion must be prevented, and justice must be administered. Where those institutional underpinnings are nonexistent or weak, as in much of the developing world, freeing up markets not only fails to deliver the expected results, but also can backfire. Privatization of state enterprises in the former Soviet Union, for example, often empowered insiders and political cronies instead of producing efficient markets. The critical assumptions behind market efficiency were obscured by the fact that advanced market economies already have strong market-supporting institutions. Western economists took them for granted.

Once their blind spot was revealed by the disappointing performance of developing and postsocialist economies, practitioners reacted in the usual way: by developing a new crop of models that underscored the importance of institutions. This was a rediscovery of an old insight: Adam Smith himself had stressed the role of the state in ensuring conditions of free competition, and economic historians like Douglass North had long pointed to improved property rights as a reason for the rise of Britain as an economic power.[7] The formalization and extension of these ideas helped economists to understand better how economic outcomes depend on the presence, variety, and shape of those institutions. Thanks to these models, the critical role that institutions play in driving economic performance has come back to the fore.

Verifying Mechanisms

Models generate conclusions by pairing assumptions with mechanisms of causation. In the oil industry example, the relationship between firms' supply and the market price is a critical mechanism: when the industry restricts supply, the market price goes up; when supply is increased, the market price goes down. Note that the models do not assume this is how the world works; they derive it as an implication. The relationship between industry supply and market prices is not an assumption, but a *result* that follows from the assumptions, in particular, that demand curves slope downward and that market prices are determined by equating the quantities demanded and supplied.

In our oil example, this is a fairly innocuous mechanism that passes the verification test comfortably. The relationship between quantities supplied and prices makes sense intuitively, and there are plenty of real-world examples in which shocks to supply have had observable effects on prices in the hypothesized direction; consider the oil shock of 1973–74, for example. We do not need to have seen a demand curve or know what the technical definition of a market equilibrium is—both abstract concepts that do not have physical counterparts—to believe that the mechanism the model relies on is reasonable. But in other cases, the mechanism may result from more complicated behavior and may require greater justification. When the justification is weak, we should be concerned about whether the model in question really applies.

Consider the Dutch disease model again. It explains how the discovery of a natural resource can harm an economy's performance through a particular channel. As a result of the resource boom, the country's exchange rate appreciates and manufacturing's profitability declines. Since manufacturing is thought to be a source of technological dynamism ("positive spillovers," in economists' parlance) for the economy as a whole, the hit that manufacturing takes translates into broader losses. The link between the real exchange rate and the health of the manufacturing sector is critical here. If we want to apply it to understand what happened in a resource-rich country, we need to convince ourselves that the manufacturing sector's position did deteriorate. If no real-world evidence supports the model's operative mechanism, the model probably isn't a good guide to what is really going on. We may need to turn to an alternative model that explains why resource booms can be bad news. For example, we may examine a model in which resource revenues induce conflict among competing elites, sparking internal strife and instability. The causal mechanism now is quite different, but it remains subject to verification.

Verifying Direct Implications

Many models are constructed to account for regularly observed phenomena. By design, their direct implications are consistent with reality. But others are built up from first principles, using the profession's preferred building blocks. They may be mathematically elegant and match up well with the prevailing modeling conventions of the day. However, this does not make them necessarily more useful, especially when their conclusions have a tenuous relationship with reality.

Macroeconomists have been particularly prone to this problem. In recent decades they have put considerable effort into developing macro models that require sophisticated mathematical tools, populated by fully rational, infinitely lived individuals solving complicated dynamic optimization problems under uncertainty. These are models that are "microfounded," in the profession's parlance: The macro-level implications are derived from the behavior of individuals, rather than simply postulated. This is a good thing, in principle. For example, aggregate saving behavior derives from the optimization problem in which a representative consumer maximizes his consumption while adhering to a lifetime (intertemporal) budget constraint.[*] Keynesian models, by contrast, take a shortcut, assuming a fixed relationship between saving and national income.

However, these models shed limited light on the classical questions of macroeconomics: Why are there economic booms and recessions? What generates unemployment? What roles can fiscal and monetary policy play in stabilizing the economy? In trying to render their models tractable, economists neglected

---

[*] An early example of these "real business cycle" (RBC) models is Finn E. Kydland and Edward C. Prescott, "Time to Build and Aggregate Fluctuations," *Econometrica* 50, no. 6 (1982): 1345–70.

many important aspects of the real world. In particular, they assumed away imperfections and frictions in markets for labor, capital, and goods. The ups and downs of the economy were ascribed to exogenous and vague "shocks" to technology and consumer preferences. The unemployed weren't looking for jobs they couldn't find; they represented a worker's optimal trade-off between leisure and labor. Perhaps unsurprisingly, these models were poor forecasters of major macroeconomic variables such as inflation and growth.[8]

As long as the economy hummed along at a steady clip and unemployment was low, these shortcomings were not particularly evident. But their failures become more apparent and costly in the aftermath of the financial crisis of 2008–9. These newfangled models simply could not explain the magnitude and duration of the recession that followed. They needed, at the very least, to incorporate more realism about financial-market imperfections. Traditional Keynesian models, despite their lack of microfoundations, could explain how economies can get stuck with high unemployment and seemed more relevant than ever. Yet the advocates of the new models were reluctant to give up on them—not because these models did a better job of tracking reality, but because they were what models were supposed to look like. Their modeling strategy trumped the realism of conclusions.

Economists' attachment to particular modeling conventions—rational, forward-looking individuals, well-functioning markets, and so on—often leads them to overlook obvious conflicts with the world around them. Yale University game theorist Barry Nalebuff is more world-savvy than most, yet even he has gotten into trouble. Nalebuff and another game theorist found themselves in a cab late one night in Israel. The driver did not turn the meter on but promised them he would charge a lower price at the end of the ride than what the meter would have indicated. Nalebuff and his colleague had no reason to trust the driver. But they were game theorists and reasoned as follows: Once they had reached their destination, the driver would have very little bargaining power. He would have to accept pretty much what his passengers were willing to pay. So they decided that the driver's offer was a good deal, and they went along. Once arriving at their destination, the driver requested 2,500 shekels. Nalebuff refused and offered 2,200 shekels instead. While Nalebuff was attempting to negotiate, the outraged driver locked the car, imprisoning his passengers inside, and drove at breakneck speed back to where he had picked them up. He kicked them to the curb, yelling, "See how far your 2,200 shekels will get you now."[9]

Standard game theory, it turned out, was a poor guide for what actually transpired. A little bit of induction may have helped Nalebuff and his colleague recognize at the outset that real-world people do not act like the rational automatons that populate theorists' models!

Today, it is unlikely they would have made the same miscalculation. Experimental work has become much more common, and game theorists have a greater appreciation of where their standard predictions go wrong. Consider the "ultimatum game," in which the calculations are reminiscent of the taxicab experience. Two players have to agree on how to share $100. One side makes a take-it-or-leave-it offer, which the other side either accepts or rejects. If the responder accepts, then each side receives what they agreed on. If he rejects, they both get nothing. If both players are "rational," the first player will keep almost the entire $100 for himself, offering the other player a tiny share (perhaps just $1). The respondent will agree, because even a token amount is better than nothing. In reality, of course, people play this game very differently. Most offers are in the range of $30–$50, and anything less is typically rejected by the responding player. Standard game theory has little predictive power for this game. That's one reason why economists have moved to different types of models. Recent work in behavioral economics incorporates considerations of fairness and therefore is more applicable to real-life settings that resemble the ultimatum game.

Lab experiments use human subjects, typically undergraduates, and have long been common in psychology. Thanks to these investigations, economists are learning more about what drives human behavior besides material self-interest, such as altruism, reciprocity, and trust. Models of competition and markets are being discarded or refined if their results are routinely violated in these experiments. But many economists remain skeptical about the value of lab experiments because of the artificial setting in which they occur. In addition, they argue, the monetary stakes for the human subjects used in the experiments are typically small, and college students may not be representative of the population at large.

One type of experiment that economists have turned to in recent years—the field experiment—is, in principle, immune to such criticisms. Typically in these experiments, economists working in concert with local organizations separate people or communities randomly into "treatment" and "control" groups and observe whether real-life outcomes differ in the manner predicted by the particular model motivating the treatment. One of the very first such experiments was attempted during the rollout in 1997 of the Mexican antipoverty program that I mentioned in the Introduction. The program—originally called *Progresa*, then *Oportunidades*, and now *Prospera*—was the front-runner of today's popular conditional cash grant programs, which provide poor families with income support as long as they keep their children in school and show up for regular health checkups. As the economist Santiago Levy, who was instrumental in designing and implementing the program, describes it, the goal was to leverage some simple economic principles to achieve better results.[10] Direct cash grants would provide more effective poverty relief than food subsidies already in place. And the conditional element of the grants would ensure, it was hoped, improved education and health.

Even though the program was national in scope, it would be phased in gradually. So, Levy got the idea that he could undertake a clean test of the effectiveness of the program. By selecting at random the communities participating in the program in the early phases, he would create separate treatment and control groups. The difference in outcomes between the two groups could then be attributed to the effects of *Progresa*. Subsequent evaluations found that *Progresa* reduced the number of people below the poverty line by 10 percent; increased boys' and girls' secondary-school enrollment rates by 8 and 14 percent, respectively; and lowered the incidence of illness in young children by about 12 percent.[11] These positive results validated the thinking that had gone into the design of the program and led governments in other countries, from Brazil to the Philippines, to institute similar conditional cash transfer programs.

Since the *Progresa* experiment, randomized field experiments have swept the field. A wide variety of social policies have been evaluated using essentially the same technique. These range from the free distribution of insecticide-treated bed nets in Kenya to the distribution of report cards to parents in Pakistan on how their children's schools are doing relative to others in the same district. Each one of these experiments is essentially a test of an underlying economic model: in Kenya, a model for the effect of small price disincentives in discouraging bed net use; and in Pakistan, a model for the role that parents empowered by better information can play in improving school performance. They have shown the powerful impact of imaginative solutions when an important constraint is identified correctly.

For example, Ted Miguel and Michael Kremer found that

a relatively cheap deworming treatment for schoolchildren in Kenya produced substantial benefits in terms of school attendance and, eventually, wages.[12] Esther Duflo, Rema Hanna, and Stephen Ryan found that placing cameras in the classroom, so that the presence of teachers could be recorded, reduced teacher absenteeism by 21 percent in rural India.[13] There were also important negative results. Field experiments to date have shown that microfinance—the provision of small loans, typically to women or groups of women—is not particularly effective in reducing poverty.[14] These results stand in sharp contrast to the hype that microfinance has attracted in development policy circles. They throw cold water on models that suggest lack of access to finance is among the most important constraints that poor households face.

MIT, Yale, and UC Berkeley have major centers devoted to running field experiments that evaluate policy and test models. The obvious shortcoming of field experiments is that they are only tenuously related to many of the central questions of economics. It is difficult to see how economy-wide experiments could be performed that would test macroeconomic questions on the role of fiscal or exchange-rate policy, for example. And, as usual, one needs to interpret experimental results with care, since those results may not apply to other settings—the usual problem of external validity.

Economists sometimes test whether their models' implications are borne out in so-called natural experiments. These experiments rely on randomness that is generated not by the researcher, but serendipitously by circumstances that have nothing to do with the research per se. One of the first such exercises in economics was MIT economist Joshua Angrist's work examining the effect of military service on men's subsequent earning ability in the labor market. To avoid the problem that men who choose to join the army may be inherently different from those who do not, Angrist used the Vietnam War–era draft lottery, which had created random recruitment. He found that men who had served in the early 1970s ended up earning about 15 percent less a decade later than men who had never served.[15]

Columbia University economists Donald Davis and David Weinstein used the US bombing of Japanese cities during the Second World War to test two models of city growth. One model was based on scale economies (decline in production costs as urban density increased), and the other was based on locational advantages (such as access to a natural seaport). Even though the bombing was obviously not random, it created a natural way to test whether cities that had been badly destroyed would remain depressed or bounce back to their original position. The model based on scale economies suggested that cities would not recover after being sharply reduced in size, whereas the locational-advantage model predicted otherwise. Davis and Weinstein found that most Japanese cities returned to their prewar relative size within a decade and a half, providing support for the latter model.[16]

Economists employ a wide a range of strategies to verify

whether the immediate implications of different models are confirmed in the real world, from the informal and anecdotal to the sophisticated and quantitative. Experimental methods generally provide more credible tests, as long as they can be carried out in settings close enough to the application in question. Many policy questions, however, either do not lend themselves to experiments or require answers in real time, thus not allowing the luxury of time-consuming field experiments. In such cases, there is no alternative to keen observation combined with common sense.

Verifying Incidental Implications

A significant advantage of having models to work with is that they provide a wide range of implications that go beyond the initial observation or motivating problem. These additional implications provide extra leverage for navigating among them. They enable the economist to move from the inductive back to the deductive mode of analysis, helping greatly in model selection.

During the mid-1990s I was investigating an empirical regularity that had received little attention in economics: countries that were more exposed to international trade had larger public sectors. This fact had been first observed by the Yale political scientist David Cameron for a subset of the member countries of the Organisation for Economic Co-operation and Development (OECD).[17] My own research showed that the finding extended also to virtually all the countries of the world (those with the requisite statistics, that is). The question was why. Cameron had hypothesized that public spending was a buffer—a source of social insurance and a stabilizer for economies that might otherwise be subjected to extensive foreign shocks. The correlation evidence was certainly consistent with this explanation.

So much for induction. But the hypothesis could be taken one step further—to ask what additional implications it had for the real world. This is where the deduction stage comes in. If Cameron's supposition was true, then the size of the public sector, upon analysis, would appear particularly sensitive to fluctuations in the economy, rather than exposure to trade per se. This implication generated an extra, more refined hypothesis that could be tested against the data. When I carried out the empirical test, looking at the effects of volatility generated by the external terms of trade (prices of exports and imports on world markets), the results fell in line. I concluded that the compensation-for-risk model had a lot going for it.[18]

My colleagues and I made considerable use of this kind of approach in our growth diagnostics work as well. We systematically looked for the tangential implications of a hypothesis to see whether they checked out. First, if an economy's prospects are undermined by bottlenecks in a particular area, the relative prices of the associated resources should be comparatively high. Shortage of physical capital (that is, plant and equipment) should show up in high real interest rates; shortage of skills should result in a high skill premium in the labor market; infrastructure constraints should produce power shortages and road congestion; and so on. Second, changes in the availability of resources in short supply should produce a particularly large response in economic activity. Investment in capital-constrained economies should respond vigorously to an inflow of remittances and other foreign funds; a similar inflow in return-constrained economies will stimulate consumption over investment.

Third, serious constraints should lead firms and households to make investments that would enable them to bypass that constraint. If electricity is in short supply, we should see lots of demand for private generators. If regulations on large firms are excessive, we should see firms taking steps to remain small. If monetary instability is a big deal, we should see a shift to foreign currencies in everyday and financial transactions ("dollarization"). Finally, firms that do relatively better should be those that rely comparatively less on the resources in short supply. As my former Harvard colleague Ricardo Hausmann likes to point out, the reason we see lots of camels and very few hippos in the desert is obvious: one animal lives in water, and the other doesn't need much water at all.* Similarly, the reason we see only skill-intensive firms doing well in an economy such as South Africa's is that unskilled labor is particularly expensive.

---

* Hausmann, Klinger, and Wagner, *Doing Growth Diagnostics in Practice*. I rely here greatly on this summary of "diagnostic signals."

External Validity, Redux

Ultimately, model selection is not unlike external validation in lab or field experiments. We have an idea that works in one setting (the model); the question is whether it also works in another (the real world). The external validity of models depends on the setting in which they're applied. Once we give up on claims of universality for our models and accept contingency, we recover their empirical relevance.

External validity is not a question that can be answered scientifically, although, as we have seen, imaginative empirical methods do help. A lot hangs on what is essentially analogical reasoning. As Robert Sugden puts it, "The gap between the model world and the real world has to be crossed by inductive inference . . . [and this] depends on subjective judgments of 'similarity,' 'salience,' and 'credibility.'"[19] While we can imagine expressing concepts such as "similarity" in formal or quantitative terms, this formalization won't be helpful in most contexts. There is an unavoidable craft element involved in rendering models useful.

CHAPTER 4

Models and Theories

You may have noticed that thus far I have generally stayed away from the word "theory." Even though "model" and "theory" are sometimes used interchangeably, not least by economists, it is best to keep them apart. The word "theory" has a ring of ambition to it. In the general definition, it refers to a collection of ideas or hypotheses put forth to explain certain facts or phenomena. In some usages, there is a presumption that it has been tested and verified; in others, it remains merely an assertion. The theory of general relativity and string theory are two examples from physics. Einstein's theory is considered to be fully borne out by subsequent experimental work. String theory, developed more recently and aimed at the unification of all forces and particles in physics, has so far received scant empirical support. Darwin's theory of evolution based on natural selection is impossible to verify directly and experimentally, in view of how long it takes for species to evolve, though there is plenty of suggestive evidence in its favor.

As with these examples from the natural sciences, a theory is presumed to be of general and universal validity. The same theory of evolution applies in both Northern and Southern Hemispheres—and might even apply to alien life. Economic models are different. They are contextual and come in almost infinite variety. They provide at best partial explanations, and they claim to be no more than abstractions designed to clarify particular mechanisms of interaction and causal channels. By leaving all potential other causes out of the analysis, these thought experiments are meant to isolate and identify the effects of a narrow set of causes. They leave us short of a full explanation of real-world phenomena when many causes might be simultaneously operating.

To see the difference between models and theories, as well as where they can overlap, we should first distinguish among three kinds of questions.

First, there are "what" questions of this sort: What is the effect of A on X? For example: What is the effect of an increase in the level of the minimum wage on employment? What is the effect of capital inflow on a country's rate of economic growth? What is the consequence of an increase in government spending on inflation? As we've seen, economic models provide answers to these questions by describing plausible causal channels and clarifying how these channels depend on a particular setting. Notice that answering these questions does not amount to making a forecast, even if we can be reasonably sure that we have the appropriate model. In the real world, many things change alongside the effect we're analyzing. We may be correct in our prediction that a rise in the minimum wage depresses employment, but in the real world the effect may be confounded by a general uptick in demand that increases employers' payrolls regardless. This kind of analysis is the proper domain of economic models.

Second, there are "why" questions that seek an explanation of an observed set of facts or developments. Why did the industrial revolution take place? Why did inequality rise in the United States after the 1970s? Why did we have the global financial crisis of 2008? In each case we can conceive of theories—and not only economic ones—that purport to provide an answer. But they are specific rather than universal theories. They aim to shed light on particular historical episodes and do not describe general laws and tendencies.

Still, the formulation of such theories poses difficulties for the analyst. An economic model scrutinizes the consequences of a particular cause. It answers what statistician Andrew Gelman calls a question of "forward causation." But explaining something after the fact requires scrutinizing all possible causes. It is, again in Gelman's terminology, a matter of "reverse causal inference." It requires looking for particular models, or some combination of models, that account for the facts under investigation. The process involves model selection and parsing of the type we saw in the previous chapter. Specific models are an essential input to the construction of such theories, as we'll see later.[1]

Finally, there are the big, timeless questions of economics and social science. What determines the distribution of income in a society? Is capitalism a stable or unstable economic system? What are the sources of social cooperation and trust, and why do they vary across societies? These questions are the domain of grand theories. A successful answer would explain the past and also provide a guide to the future. To that extent, these theories would form the social analogue of the physical laws of nature. Contemporary economics is often criticized for not taking on these big questions. Where is today's Karl Marx or Adam Smith? Would they even get tenure at a half-decent university? These are fair criticisms. But a reasonable counter-argument would be that universal theories are impossible to formulate in the social sciences, and that the best we can do is come up with a series of contingent explanations.

Economics does have its general theories—particular models that make ambitious claims about their explanatory power over the workings of market-based societies. These can be a source of great clarification, as we'll see. But I will argue that general economic theories are no more than a scaffolding for empirical contingencies. They are a way of organizing our thoughts, rather than stand-alone explanatory frameworks. On their own, they have little real leverage over the world. They need to be combined with considerable contextual analysis before they become useful.

I will then turn to theories of the intermediate kind, meant to explain particular developments in the economy. I focus on a concrete question: Why has inequality increased in the United States so much since the 1970s? We will assess the relative contributions of different models and show how such a process generates insight even when it does not produce a conclusive and widely agreed theory.

The Theory of Value and Its Distribution

Perhaps the most fundamental question in economics is, What creates value? For an economist, this means: What explains the prices of different goods and services in a market economy? The "theory of value" in economics is essentially a theory about price formation. If this question no longer seems foundational—or particularly interesting—for the contemporary reader, it is because it has been demystified by theoretical developments that cut through a thicket of confusion surrounding it.

Classical economists such as Adam Smith, David Ricardo, and Karl Marx subscribed to the view that the costs of production determined value. If something costs more to produce, its price must be higher. Costs of production were, in turn, traced to wage payments made to workers, either directly in the activity in question or indirectly when labor was employed to produce the machines that were being used. This was dubbed the "labor theory of value," to be distinguished from earlier theories, like that of the French physiocrats, who viewed land as the ultimate source of value.

But it is one thing to say labor creates value and another to explain the level of wages. Classical economists tended to have a pretty dreary view on that. They presumed wages would hover around the subsistence level, the level required to feed, clothe, and shelter a family. If wages rose too much above this level, the result would be an increase in population—because more children could survive—and in the labor force. As a consequence, wages would drop back down to their "natural" level. The main beneficiaries of economic advances and technological progress would therefore be owners of land, which was in finite supply. It was this kind of thinking, associated in particular with Thomas Malthus, that led the nineteenth-century essayist Thomas Carlyle to famously call economics the "dismal science."

Marx, whose influence would extend well into the twentieth century, also adhered to the labor theory of value. He, too, believed that wages were held down. But in his theory the culprits were capitalists who exploited workers and managed to discipline them through the "reserve army of the unemployed." In Marx's case, capitalists expropriated the surplus value from workers' efforts. But this was a Pyrrhic victory, as competition among capitalists would eventually drive the profit rate down and invite a generalized crisis of the capitalist system.

The labor theory of value, placing the onus of price determination solely on the production side, had little to say about consumers. But didn't the demand side of the picture play a role? Shouldn't prices also respond to the preferences of consumers and any changes in those preferences? The classical approach focused on the long run. It had little to say on short-run fluctuations or on the determination of *relative* prices.

The full synthesis of the supply and demand sides of price determination came with the "marginalist" revolution of the late nineteenth century. Marginalist economists such as William Stanley Jevons, Léon Walras, Eugen von Böhm-Bawerk, Alfred Marshall, Knut Wicksell, and John Bates Clark shifted the ground of analysis one step back: from observed quantities such as wages and rents toward unobserved hypothetical mathematical constructs such as "consumer's utility" and "production functions." They also generalized the classical approach by allowing substitution among different production inputs such as labor and capital; they could now analyze how firms switch from, say, labor to machines as wages and machine prices changed. Their use of explicit mathematical relationships enabled them to describe the determination of prices, costs, and quantities in different markets as the simultaneous outcome of (and interplay between) consumer preferences and the state of production technology.

The marginalists established a chief insight of the modern theory of value—namely, that prices are determined at the margin. What determines the market price of oil, for example, is not the production cost or consumer valuation of oil *on aver-*

age. It is the cost and valuation of the *last unit* of oil sold. In market equilibrium, the production cost and consumer valuation of that last unit (the marginal unit) are exactly equal—to each other and to the market price. If they were not, the market would not be in equilibrium and there would be adjustments to bring these back into equilibrium. When the market price exceeds consumers' valuation of the last unit, consumers cut back on their purchases; when it falls short, consumers buy more. Similarly, when the market price is greater than the cost of producing the last unit, firms expand production; when it is less, firms reduce production.

The marginalists discovered that the supply and demand curves represent none other than the marginal costs and marginal valuations of the producers and consumers, respectively. The market price is where these two schedules intersect. The answer to the question of whether value is determined by production costs or, alternatively, by consumer benefits is that it is determined by both—at the margin.

The marginalists' approach to determining prices applied equally well to costs of production. Labor's earnings (wages) are determined by the marginal productivity of labor, and capitalists' earnings (rents) are determined by the marginal product of capital—what the last unit of labor and capital, respectively, add to the output of the firm. Now, suppose that production takes place under constant returns, meaning that doubling the amount of capital and labor used doubles the amount of output. Under this assumption, the math guarantees that paying labor, capital, and other inputs their marginal productivity results in a full allocation of the income generated by production among all the inputs that contribute to production. In other words, we now have a theory of distribution—who gets what—in addition to a theory of value.

This theory tells us how national income is distributed between labor and capital. If we distinguish further among different types of labor, we can also get the distribution of income across workers of various skill types, such as high school dropouts, high school graduates, and college graduates. This is what's called the functional distribution of income. By combining it with information on the type and amount of capital people own, we can, in turn, derive the distribution of income across individuals or households—the personal distribution of income.

How useful are such theories? On the face of it, the neoclassical synthesis appears to provide solid answers to two of the fundamental questions in economics: What creates value, and what determines how it is distributed? These theories have clarified a lot. In particular, we now understand how production, consumption, and prices are all jointly determined as a system. And we have a plausible account of the functional distribution of income. But the theories are based on concepts—marginal utility, marginal cost, marginal product—that cannot be observed. They require additional assumptions and considerably more structure before they can be made operational in the sense of measurement and explanation. Furthermore, they are far from universal. Subsequent research has made clear that, even within their own logic, these theories depend on special circumstances.

We've already seen how the supply-demand framework on which value theory rests is subject to important caveats. The conditions for perfect competition may not exist, and the market may be monopolized by a small number of producers. Consumers may behave in ways that are far from rational. Production may be subject to scale economies, and marginal costs may decrease with quantities produced, contradicting the rising marginal costs required for the standard upward-sloping supply curve. And in any case, where do concepts such as the "production function" and "utility" come from? Firms clearly differ in their ability to access, adopt, and employ available technologies. Consumer preferences are hardly fixed; they are shaped in part by what happens in the economic and social world. Opening up these particular black boxes creates new theoretical challenges that are not yet fully resolved.

The neoclassical theory of distribution has its own special holes. For one thing, the notion of a coherent, measurable concept of "capital" as a unified factor of production has been the source of considerable controversy within the profession. But let's set that thorny issue aside. Focusing on wages alone, does the marginal-productivity theory track the behavior of labor compensation?

The answer is that it depends on the precise question and the setting we're examining. Looking across countries, between 80 and 90 percent of the differences in wage levels can be accounted for by the variation in national labor productivity levels. We do not observe marginal productivity directly; all we can measure is average labor productivity (gross domestic product divided by employment levels). But as long as the relationship between the average and the marginal does not vary much across nations, the tight cross-country association between wages and average labor productivity can be interpreted as supporting the theory. This is not a trivial matter. It allows us to conclude, for example, that wages in Bangladesh or Ethiopia are a small fraction of wages in the United States largely because of the poor state of productivity in these countries—and not because of the exploitation of labor or coercive institutions. Institutions might matter, but they seem to be directly responsible for at most a small share of the variation across countries in distributive outcomes between labor and capital.[2]

But let's look at what has happened in the United States since 2000. Average real compensation grew by about 1 percent per year between 2000 and 2011, from about $32 per hour to $35 per hour (in 2011 dollars). Meanwhile, labor productivity grew by 1.9 percent per year during the same period, at almost twice the growth rate of compensation. Some of this gap is due to the fact that the prices of the goods US workers consume rose more rapidly than the prices of goods they produce. So the consuming power of workers increased less rapidly than their productivity—something that can be accommodated within the standard theory without a great stretch. This relative-price effect, however, accounts for only about a quarter of the gap, leaving the remaining three-quarters a mystery.[*]

To remain strictly within the boundaries of neoclassical distribution theory, we would have to say that labor's marginal contribution to output fell sharply in this period. One possible culprit is the increasing use of machines and other forms of capital, as well as the displacement of labor by new technologies. Indeed, many economists make this argument when interpreting the weak growth in wages over the last decade. But the same result may also have been due to changes outside the ambit of neoclassical theory—in bargaining, workplace norms, and policies such as minimum wages. Distinguishing among these alternative explanations is difficult because the neoclassical theory hinges on the mathematical representation of the underlying technology (the "production function") and the changes therein, which are not directly observable. Ultimately, a theory that cannot be pinned down is not very helpful.

A wide variety of alternative theories of distribution exist. Some emphasize explicit bargaining between employers and employees, where the prevalence of trade unions and collective-bargaining rules can shape the sharing of revenues of the enterprise between the two parties. Compensation levels of high income earners such as CEOs seem also to be deter-

[*] Lawrence Mishel, *The Wedges between Productivity and Median Compensation Growth*, Issue Brief 330 (Washington, DC: Economic Policy Institute, 2012). Mishel focuses on *median* wages, which have increased considerably more slowly than average wages, because of rising inequality in compensation.

mined largely by bargaining.[3] Other models highlight the role of norms in the spread that is considered acceptable between, say, the CEO's compensation and the amounts earned by rank-and-file employees. Most economists would acknowledge that workers in the United States and Europe greatly benefited from the more egalitarian social understanding of the 1950s and 1960s. Yet other models suggest that profit-maximizing reasons motivate certain firms to pay more than the going market wage, without departing from the marginal-productivity framework as such. For example, above-market "efficiency" wages, as they are called, may make sense for employers in order to motivate workers or minimize labor turnover (to reduce costs of hiring and training). These wrinkles move us away from general-purpose models and take us back, again, to specific models that may be relevant in different settings.

The big theories in the end deliver less than what they promise. They are shallow approaches that identify the proximate causes but need to be backed up with considerable detail, necessarily specific to context. As I've highlighted, they are best thought of as a scaffolding.

The Theory of Business Cycles and Unemployment

Ever since Paul Samuelson's doctoral dissertation, published in 1947 as *Foundations of Economic Analysis*, economics has been split between microeconomics and macroeconomics. The domain of microeconomics is price theory, the ideas covered in the previous section. Macroeconomics deals with the behavior of economic aggregates—inflation, total output, and employment, in particular. Macroeconomics takes as its central questions the up-and-down fluctuations in economic activity that economists call the "business cycle." Here, too, there has been no shortage of grand theorizing. We have learned considerably with each successive wave. But the attempts to develop a grand unified theory of what determines the business cycle have to be judged a failure.

To classical economists, there was not much difference between the way individual markets worked and the way the economy as a whole behaved. Unemployment, in particular, could be understood as a result of wages (the market price of labor) being set at the wrong level. If wages were too high, employers would hire too few workers, just as too high a price for apples would result in too little apple consumption. This scenario has come to be called "classical unemployment." Along similar lines, the overall level of prices in the economy was determined by the quantity of money and liquidity in the system. Sustained price inflation was the result of too much money being in circulation.

The classical economists' approach to the business cycle was typified by their view that the macroeconomy, to use the term anachronistically, was self-stabilizing. Unemployment would eventually be eliminated as the shortage of jobs brought wages down. A burst of inflation similarly would be cured on its own: the resultant loss in international competitiveness would produce a trade deficit, financed by the outflow of gold abroad, which in turn would lead to a corrective reduction in the domestic money supply. These supposedly automatic adjustment mechanisms ensured that the business cycle, inflation, and unemployment would all take care of themselves. The Gold Standard epitomized this economic orthodoxy and stood well into the twentieth century. Under Gold Standard rules, countries fixed their currencies' value against gold. For example, in the United States the price of gold stood unchanged at $20.67 per ounce between 1834 and 1933.[*] Governments renounced any interference in the free flow of money across their borders, effectively placing their monetary policy on economic autopilot. There was no concept of fiscal policy or stabilization policy as we know them today. Governments could (and should) do nothing, except to stay out of the way of these adjustments.

John Maynard Keynes thought otherwise. A conservative revolutionary, he formulated doctrines that aimed to save capitalism from what he felt were its inherent instabilities. Keynes argued that it was possible for an economy with unemployment to remain in an equilibrium for a considerable stretch of time. The classical adjustment mechanisms would take too long to

---

[*] With the exception of the interlude during the greenback era from 1861 to 1878. Michael D. Bordo, "The Classical Gold Standard: Some Lessons for Today," *Federal Reserve Bank of St. Louis Review*, May 1981, 2–17.

work themselves out—years, perhaps even decades, and in the long run, as he famously put it, "we are all dead." Moreover, Keynes argued, there was plenty that the government could do. When private demand fell short of what was required to generate sufficient employment, Keynes contended, it should step in and increase fiscal spending. Even if the expansion of government programs led to people digging ditches and then filling them back in, the net result would be fuller employment and rising national income. The Great Depression gave great currency to these ideas, as governments found themselves forced to respond to catastrophic spells of unemployment, which in the United States peaked at a quarter of the labor force.

Keynes was an exceptionally good and witty writer, but he did not formulate explicit models, and his reasoning was sometimes cloudy. To this day, economic historians debate what the great theorist really meant by this or that. The ink on his magnum opus, *The General Theory of Employment, Interest, and Money* (published in 1936), was barely dry before models trying to encapsulate the Keynesian framework began to appear. Among these, the most famous, and the one that had the greatest impact for decades, was John Hicks's "Mr. Keynes and the 'Classics.'"[4] Hicks's model was the vehicle through which Keynes's views transformed standard macroeconomics—despite the protests of many, including Keynes, that it was at best a partial representation of the *General Theory*. Keynes was, in fact, explicit that he was not interested in crafting a model of his ideas. He thought it more important to communicate some "comparatively simple fundamental ideas" than to crystallize them in particular forms.[5]

Crucial to the Keynesian apparatus was the possibility of an imbalance between saving and investment in the economy. These two have to equal each other after the fact, as a matter of accounting identity: whatever is saved must find its way into investment, and all investment has to be financed by saving (ignoring what can be borrowed from or lent to other countries). But Keynes highlighted the possibility that the mechanism through which the identity is restored could introduce unemployment into the economy. Suppose, for concreteness, the amount that households desire to save initially exceeds investment. Keynes thought investment is determined by psychological factors ("animal spirits") that are largely external to macroeconomic variables such as interest rates. If the investment level is somehow fixed by other considerations, it is saving that must adjust. How does saving come down, then, to the lower level required by the equality between investment and saving?

Classical economists offering a response would emphasize the role of price adjustments, including the interest rate. A decline in the level of prices, or a fall in the interest rate, would boost households' incentives to consume and eventually lower savings. Keynes thought such price changes would be too slow, especially in the downward direction. He highlighted instead adjustments in the level of aggregate output and employment. Since household saving depends on the household's income, a reduction in output (and therefore incomes and employment) also lowers saving and brings it closer to equality with investment. Moreover, in situations of economic depression, where unemployment has shot up, people may want to hoard money so much that the interest rate becomes essentially insensitive to changes in economic circumstances. This is the Keynesian "liquidity trap." In this scenario the adjustment can arrive only through a sufficiently large drop in output and employment. The high level of saving among individual households proves, collectively, self-defeating. Recession follows.

In this model of autonomous changes in aggregate demand, business cycle fluctuations are the result. Insufficient demand is the fundamental cause of unemployment. An increase in private investment or consumption spending, were it to happen, would fix the problem. In the absence of either, the government has to act: fiscal spending must be raised to make up for lack of private demand. This demand-side view of macroeconomics prevailed pretty much through the 1970s. It was elaborated in models of increasing variety and spawned large-scale computerized versions that could generate quantitative forecasts of major macroeconomic aggregates such as employment levels and capacity utilization rates.

Then two things happened: the oil shock and Robert Lucas. The oil crisis of 1973, precipitated by the embargo applied by the Organization of the Petroleum Exporting Countries (OPEC), fomented a new set of economic circumstances that had not been on economists' radar screen: recession and inflation at the same time, or "stagflation." Demand-side models wouldn't be much help in the face of what was patently a supply-side shock. Of course, the Keynesian model could be tweaked to accommodate the effect of a rise in input prices. Many attempts were made to do just that. But then Lucas, the University of Chicago economist and future Nobel Prize winner, came along with a set of ideas that revolutionized the field of macroeconomics and eventually did much greater damage to the Keynesian model.

At the close of the 1970s, Lucas reintroduced classical thinking into macroeconomics, in a new guise. Along with others (in particular Tom Sargent, then at the University of Minnesota), Lucas argued that Keynesian models took a far too mechanical view of how individuals behave in the economy and how they respond to government policies.[6] In the words of John Cochrane, another Chicago economist, Lucas and Sargent put people back into macroeconomics.[7] Instead of relying on aggregate relationships between, say, consumption and income, they began to model how individuals decide to consume, save, and supply labor in much the same way that microeconomics had traditionally done, but they extended those models to macrobehavior. These became the "microfoundations" of a larger theory.

This change in modeling strategy had a couple of important implications. One is that it brought budget constraints explicitly into the picture, both for individuals and for the government. Private consumption depends on future income as well as current income, and government deficits today imply higher taxes (or lower government spending) tomorrow. The strategy also forced a reconsideration of how expectations are formed. If people are rational in making their consumption decisions, Lucas and Sargent argued, they should also be rational in how they make their forecasts about the future. These forecasts should be consistent with the underlying model of the economy—hence the hypothesis of "rational expectations," which took the profession by storm. Rational expectations quickly became the benchmark in the modeling of expectations, which economists use to analyze the reaction of the private sector to changes in government policy, among other questions.

Lucas, Sargent, and their followers argued that such micro-founded models could account for the main features of business cycles and generate temporary unemployment without relying on Keynesian assumptions such as sluggish adjustment in prices. Rational expectations implied that people did not make predictable errors, but it did not rule out temporary mistakes when people had incomplete information about prices. "Shocks" to consumer tastes, employment preferences, or technological conditions—that is, to demand and supply curves—could generate aggregate fluctuations in output and employment. Equally important, the new theory implied that the government's influence in stabilizing the economy was much weaker. In fact, any kind of stabilization policy would produce perverse outcomes. When people knew the government had a policy of stimulating the economy through monetary and fiscal expansion, they would behave in ways that would defeat the purpose of such policies. For example, activist monetary policy would lead firms to raise their prices, producing inflation with no gains in terms of output and employment. Fiscal stimulus would only lead to crowding out—cutbacks in spending on the part of the private sector.

What made the "new classical approach," as it came to be called, a winner—at least in academia—was not its empirical validation. The real-world fit of the model was heavily contested, as was the realism of some of the key ingredients. But shortly after the arrival of the new theory, in the mid-1980s the US economy entered a period of economic growth, full employment, and price stability. The business cycle looked to be conquered in this era of "great moderation." As a result, the descriptive and predictive realism of the new classical approach seemed, from a practical perspective, not to matter a whole lot.

The great appeal of the theory lay in the model itself. The microfoundations, the math, the new techniques, the close links to game theory, econometrics, and other highly regarded fields within economics—all these made the new macroeconomics appear light-years ahead of Keynesian models. "This is what macroeconomic models are supposed to look like" was the implicit or explicit rebuke to anyone who would question the strategy beneath the model. Meanwhile, the Keynesian modeling apparatus deriving from Hicks became virtually extinct. But Keynesianism did not disappear altogether. Those who thought active government policy retained a role in stabilizing the economy were ultimately forced to develop variants of microfounded models, called new Keynesian models, to retain credibility within the discipline.

The disconnect between the new classical theory and the real economy came home to roost in the aftermath of the global financial crisis of 2008. Why economists failed to see the crisis coming is the subject of the next chapter. The crisis was instigated largely by failures in the financial system; the Keynesian and new classical macro models alike were mute on such matters. But once the US economy sank into recession and unemployment took off, the question of appropriate remedies was—or should have been—squarely the province of macroeconomics. Yet the prevailing macro models, descendants of the Lucas-Sargent approach, offered little help. Writing in early 2003, Lucas had said, "[The] central problem of depression prevention has been solved, for all practical purposes."[8] In the intervening years not much thought had gone into fighting a great recession, because there wouldn't be one.

On one thing, the new and old models agreed. When economic uncertainty produces a sudden flight to safety in that households and firms hoard as much cash as they can, the Federal Reserve should produce additional liquidity by printing money—lots of it. Increasing the amount of money in circulation prevents deflation and a more severe recession. Milton Friedman had pointed out many years earlier that failure to act in this way was the Fed's biggest mistake during the Great Depression of the 1930s. When the Fed's Ben Bernanke, an expert on the Depression, injected hundreds of billions of dollars of liquidity into the economy in 2008–9, Lucas applauded the action.[9] President Obama's initial fiscal stimulus package of 2009 also received widespread support (including from Lucas), even if viewed as a desperate, last-resort measure.*

Beyond these measures, and once the financial panic subsided, the new classical models suggested restraint and caution and not much else. The Fed's policies of quantitative easing—its monetary expansion—had to be withdrawn quickly; otherwise, it soon would lead to inflation. Economists trained on these models kept warning about the dangers of inflation and urged the Fed to tighten its policy, even though unemployment remained high, the economy performed below par, and—notably —inflation refused to appear. They argued against continued fiscal stimulus to lift aggregate demand and employment, since such measures would only crowd out private consumption and investment. The economy would get back on track largely

* Holman W. Jenkins Jr., "Chicago Economics on Trial" (interview with Robert E. Lucas), *Wall Street Journal*, September 24, 2011, http://online.wsj.com/news/articles/SB100014240531119041946045765833 82550849232. In a survey of thirty-seven leading economists in 2014, all except one agreed that the stimulus had reduced unemployment, and the majority thought the benefits of the package exceeded its costs. Justin Wolfers, "What Debate? Economists Agree the Stimulus Lifted the Economy," The Upshot, *New York Times*, July 29, 2014, http://www.nytimes.com/2014/07/30/upshot/what-debate-economists-agree-the-stimulus-lifted-the-economy.html?rref=upshot.

on its own. When this failed to happen, Lucas and others fingered obstacles put in place by the Democratic administration. The sluggish recovery was due to uncertainty created by the prospect of higher taxes and other government interventions, they claimed.[10] Businesses failed to invest and consumers failed to spend because they faced an artificial climate of uncertainty created by an activist government.

To many others, the recession vindicated Keynes's original ideas. The economist and *New York Times* columnist Paul Krugman was vociferous in arguing that the fiscal stimulus was inadequate and had been withdrawn too soon, condemning the economy to unnecessarily high and prolonged levels of unemployment.[11] Brad DeLong and Larry Summers, from UC Berkeley and Harvard, respectively, argued that concerns about the deficit were misplaced; fiscal stimulus would actually pay for itself as it helped the economy recover.[12] These are all well-known and distinguished economists. Krugman had won a Nobel Prize for his pioneering work of introducing imperfect competition into the theory of international trade. Summers had served as secretary of the treasury in the Obama administration. But they were outsiders to the new classical models that had come to dominate the discipline.

The main bone of contention between the Keynesians and the new classicals was whether the problems were on the demand or the supply side of the economy. In principle, economists had ways to discriminate between the competing ideas and choose the more relevant ones. The principles of model selection discussed in the previous chapter are tailor-made for such a project. Keynesians, reasonably enough, pointed out that if the problem was a shortfall in supply, there would be evidence of inflationary pressures and there was none. Unemployment seemed to affect all sectors of the economy and was not related to the specific circumstances of each industry, again pointing to a generalized collapse in demand as the culprit.[13] The other side, meanwhile, presented evidence from news articles, changes in the tax code, and forecaster disagreements that policy uncertainty had risen and seemed to explain at least a portion of the increase in unemployment and decline in economic growth, both over time and across US states.[14] It is not clear whether the evidence swayed anyone's prior opinions in the debate. When conviction in the relevance of a theory is strong, as in this case, empirical analysis hardly settles matters—especially when the analysis has to be carried out in real time.

What can we conclude about these grand theories of the business cycle? Certainly they have not been pointless. Classical, Keynesian, and new classical theories each make useful contributions. The Keynesian approach had little relevance to the experience of the 1970s, but many of its insights remain valid and useful today. The new classical approach has made us more cognizant of the need to understand how individuals will respond to government policies. Where these have failed is as grand theories that apply at all times, regardless of circumstances. As models that are specific to particular settings, they remain immensely valuable.

Theories as Explanation of Specific Events

Let's turn now to the intermediate kind of economic theory that I mentioned at the beginning of the chapter. Less ambitious in scope, it seeks to uncover the causes of a particular set of developments. It makes no claim to provide a generic explanation for all developments of a similar type. It is typically historically and geographically specific.

The specific example I will consider here is the theories behind the rise in inequality in the United States and some other advanced economies since the late 1970s. Even if widely accepted, these theories are not meant to apply to other settings. The explanations I will consider do not attempt to account also for, say, the rise of inequality in this country during the gilded age before World War I or the decline in inequality in many Latin American countries since the 1990s. They are *sui generis*.

The steep rise in US inequality that began in the mid-1970s is well documented. The Gini coefficient, a widely used measure of inequality that varies from 0 (no inequality) to 1 (maximum inequality, with all income going to a single household), rose from 0.40 in 1973 to 0.48 in 2012—a 20 percent increase.[15] The country's richest 10 percent raised their share of national income from 32 to 48 percent over the same period.[16] What caused this dramatic change?

One factor behind the rise in inequality was an increase in the "skill premium," the gap between what high- and low-skilled workers earn. When economists first homed in on this gap beginning in the late 1980s, there was a plausible explanation at hand: globalization. The US economy had become much more exposed to international trade in recent years. Other advanced economies in Europe and Japan had largely caught up with the United States in productivity and now offered stiff competition. And there were many newly rising exporters in East Asia—South Korea, Taiwan, China—where wages were a fraction of the US level.

Since Ricardo's days there had been many elaborations of the Principle of Comparative Advantage. The reigning version of the theory, called the "factor endowments" theory and first articulated by Eli Heckscher and Bertil Ohlin in the early twentieth century, predicted precisely the kinds of changes in relative wages that were taking place in the United States. According to the theory, the country would be exporting goods that were intensive in skilled labor and importing goods that were intensive in unskilled labor. Greater openness to international trade was good news for American skilled workers, who could now access larger markets, but bad news for low-skilled workers, who had to put up with greater competition. As UCLA economist Edward Leamer put it in the early 1990s, "Our low-skill workers face a sea of low-paid, low-skilled workers around the world."[17] As a consequence, the gap between the wages of the two types of workers would increase. In fact, the theory had an even stronger implication. Unskilled workers would lose out not just in relative but also in absolute terms. Increased open-ness would reduce their living standards.*

Discussion might have rested there, but economists noticed other developments that seemed incompatible with the factor endowments theory. For one thing, the skill premium was also rising in the United States' low-wage trade partners in Asia and Latin America. This was a problem for the theory because it had predicted a movement in the skill premium in the opposite direction in those countries. Unskilled workers should have benefited through higher wages in countries exporting low-skill-intensive goods. And in the United States, individual industries were defying the theory's predictions. Firms were substituting skilled labor for unskilled labor—there was skill upgrading—when they should have been doing the reverse if trade had caused unskilled labor to become cheaper.[18] This was a good example of how economists could use the incidental implications of a model to verify, or in this case disprove, a specific explanation.

These conflicting findings did not necessarily rule out glo-balization as a driver of rising inequality. But they did imply that if globalization was the real cause, it must have operated through channels other than those highlighted by the factor endowments theory. An alternative globalization-based model

* This is the consequence of the Stolper-Samuelson theorem, an extension of the factor endowments theory. Wolfgang Stolper and Paul A. Samuelson, "Protection and Real Wages," *Review of Economic Studies* 9, no. 1 (1941): 58–73.

soon coalesced around foreign investment and offshoring. Industrial operations depend on the production of many different components. Suppose, reasonably, that the most skill-intensive parts of an industry are manufactured in the United States, while the least skill-intensive parts are manufactured in a developing country such as Mexico. As globalization renders offshoring easier by reducing tariff, transport, and communication costs, US firms move some of their production to Mexico. It can be expected that the components that are offshored will be, for US firms, among the least skill-intensive. But the same components, when produced in Mexico, will be among the most skill-intensive there. As a result, somewhat paradoxically, industries in both the United States and Mexico experience skill upgrading. Relative demand for skilled workers rises in both countries, as does the risk premium. Rob Feenstra and Gordon Hanson, who first advanced this hypothesis, showed that evidence from Mexican maquiladoras—manufacturing plants operating in the country's free-trade zones—was consistent with the model.[19]

The main alternative to the globalization thesis was technological change. This was an age of rapid advances in information and communication technologies and the spread of computers. Normally, broad technological progress that increases labor productivity is expected to improve everyone's living standards. But some may benefit more than others. The new technologies required skilled workers to operate them, so the demand for those with college education or higher rose much more rapidly than the demand for less skilled workers. This was "skill-biased technological change" (SBTC), as economists called it.[20]

The SBTC hypothesis explained the rise in the skill premium. In addition, unlike the factor endowments model, it was consistent with skill upgrading within firms and industries. Employers were hiring more skilled workers as a result of automation and greater use of computers. Since these technological changes were sweeping the rest of the world as well, the theory also accounted for rising wage inequality in developing nations. By the end of the 1990s, a near-consensus had emerged among trade and labor economists that SBTC was the primary culprit behind the increase in the skill premium. Trade may have played a role, but it accounted for no more than 10–20 percent of the trend.

Doubts crept in before too long. The skill premium had stabilized during the 1990s, even though the introduction of new technologies had not slowed down. (It would start to rise again, with a vengeance, in the 2000s.) Many of the developments in wages could not be explained by SBTC alone. For example, wage inequality grew significantly within skill categories as well, such as among college graduates. The upgrading of jobs and the rise in the share of high-skill occupations had been taking place since at least the 1950s, without necessarily producing inequality. Even if technological changes were somehow behind all these trends, wasn't it possible that increased globalization was the stimulus behind the new technologies introduced after the 1970s? Finally, an important part of the rise in equality had to do with the growth of incomes at the very top of the income distribution—the top 1 percent. A substantial part of that upward trend, in turn, derived from capital income (returns on stocks and bonds) rather than wages.

These concerns made it unlikely that SBTC on its own could account for what was happening with inequality. A third, catchall category of explanations focused on the wide range of policy and attitudinal changes that had taken place from the late 1970s on. Macroeconomic policy became more concerned about price stability and less focused on full employment. Trade unions shrank, workers lost bargaining power, and the minimum wage was allowed to lag behind prices. Workplace norms that precluded large wage dispersion—the gap between the highest and lowest paid employees—became weaker. Deregulation and the vast expansion of the finance sector enabled the amassing of fortunes that would have been unthinkable decades ago.[21]

In the end, it was clear that no single theory could fully explain the story of US inequality since the 1970s. Nor was there a good way of parsing the relative contributions of different theories. Certain theories (models) gave us a better understanding of the channels through which trade, technology, and other factors may have operated. The failure of other theories allowed us to rule out mechanisms that appeared equally plausible at the outset. There was no closure, but there was plenty of learning along the way.

Theories Are Really Just Models

As we've seen, theories in economics are either so general that they have little real leverage in the real world or so specific that they can account at best for a particular slice of reality. I have illustrated this conundrum with specific theories, but the point is valid for other areas in economics as well. History has not been kind to theorists who claimed to have discovered the universal laws of capitalism. Unlike nature, capitalism is a human, and therefore malleable, construction.

Yet judging by the frequency with which the term "theory" is used, economics is full of theories. There is game theory, contract theory, search theory, growth theory, monetary theory, and so on. But do not be fooled by the terminology. In reality, each one of these is simply a particular collection of models, to be applied judiciously and with due care to setting. Each serves as a tool kit rather than an all-purpose explanation of the phenomena it studies. As long as more is not expected of them, these theories can be quite useful and relevant.

Nearly half a century ago, Albert Hirschman, one of economics' most creative minds, complained about social scientists' "compulsion to theorize" and described how the search for grand paradigms could be a "hindrance to understanding."[22] The urge to formulate all-encompassing theories, he feared, would blind scholars to the role of contingency and the variety of possibilities that the real world threw their way. Much of what happens in the world of economics these days does reflect a more modest goal: the search for understanding one cause at a time. When ambition eclipses this aim, trouble often looms.

CHAPTER 5

When Economists Go Wrong

I t is probably the shortest graduation speech on record. When macroeconomist Tom Sargent stepped up to the podium at UC Berkeley's graduation ceremony in May 2007, he said he found such speeches too long. He got right to the heart of the matter. Economics, he said, is "organized common sense." He went on to list twelve items that he said "our beautiful subject teaches." The first was, "Many things that are desirable are not feasible." The second, "Individuals and communities face trade-offs." By the fourth item, Sargent was on to the role of the government: "Everyone responds to incentives. . . . That is why social safety nets don't always end up working as intended." Next item: "There are tradeoffs between equality and efficiency," by which he meant that governments could improve the distribution of income only at some economic cost.[1]

Sargent probably thought his list was uncontroversial.

Indeed, his speech would earn plaudits from economists at both ends of the political spectrum. But there were dissenters, such as the economist and blogger Noah Smith. By the end of the list, Smith complained, ten of Sargent's twelve lessons were "cautions against trying to use government to promote equality or help people." Paul Krugman was critical as well. He chided Sargent for trying to pass off as universal truths ideas that applied only to a well-functioning market economy at full employment. Take Sargent's observation about the trade-off between equality and efficiency. Smith wrote that there was, in fact, no such trade-off under one of economics' benchmark assumptions (that transfers among individuals can take place without causing inefficiency). Krugman pointed to recent empirical research that suggested high inequality might hamper economic growth.[2]

Sargent's critics were right. Beyond trite generalities such as "incentives matter" or "beware unintended consequences," there are few immutable truths in economics. All the valuable lessons that the "beautiful profession" teaches are contextual. They are if-then statements in which the "if" matters as much as the "then."

But Sargent did accurately summarize what *economists* tend to think. Smith and Krugman notwithstanding, most economists do believe, to continue with the same example, that there is a trade-off between equity and efficiency. Mind you, these same economists are fully aware that certain models (and some evidence) point in the opposite direction. But their existence does not seem to stand in the way of a categorical near-consensus.

There are, in fact, many important matters on which nearly all professional economists agree. Greg Mankiw, the Harvard professor and author of a leading economics textbook, provided a list in his blog a few years back.[3] Here are some of the top ones (the numbers in parentheses indicate the percentage of economists who agree with the proposition).

1. A ceiling on rents reduces the quantity and quality of housing available. (93%)

2. Tariffs and import quotas usually reduce general economic welfare. (93%)

3. Flexible and floating exchange rates offer an effective international monetary arrangement. (90%)

4. Fiscal policy (for example, tax cuts and/or government expenditure increases) has a significant stimulative impact on a less than fully employed economy. (90%)

5. The United States should not restrict employers from outsourcing work to foreign countries. (90%)

6. The United States should eliminate agricultural subsidies. (85%)

7. A large federal budget deficit has an adverse effect on the economy. (83%)

8. A minimum wage increases unemployment among young and unskilled workers. (79%)

Unless you skipped the previous chapters, the degree of consensus on these propositions should surprise you. For at least four of the eight, we have already seen models that contradict them. Rent controls (ceilings on what landlords can charge) do not necessarily restrict the supply of housing if landlords behave monopolistically, trade restrictions do not necessarily reduce efficiency, fiscal stimulus does not necessarily work, and minimum wages do not necessarily raise unemployment. In all of these cases, there are models with imperfect competition, imperfect markets, or imperfect information where the reverse outcome prevails. The same is true of Mankiw's other propositions as well.

What economics teaches us are the explicit conditions—critical assumptions—under which one conclusion or its opposite is correct. Yet virtually all the economists surveyed (90 percent or more) are apparently willing to vouch for the general validity of a particular set of critical assumptions. Perhaps they stick their necks out because they believe those assumptions are more common in the real world. Or they think one set of models works better "on average" than any other. Even so, as scientists, should they not adorn their endorsements with the appropriate caveats? Shouldn't they worry that such categorical statements have the potential to mislead?

We have arrived at one of the central paradoxes of economics: uniformity amid diversity. Economists work with a plethora of models, pointing in all kinds of contradictory directions. Yet when it comes to the issues of the day, their views often converge in ways that cannot be justified by the strength of the available evidence.

Let me be clear: Economists are constantly debating vigorously on a variety of issues. What should the top income tax rate be? Should the minimum wage be raised? Are patents important for stimulating innovation? On these and many other issues, economists often see both sides. Frustrated by the conflicting and hedged advice he was receiving from his advisers, President Harry S. Truman is said to have asked for a "one-handed economist." "If all the *economists* were laid end to end, they'd still not reach a conclusion," George Bernard Shaw once supposedly quipped. An economists' consensus is perhaps more a rarity than a regularity. But when it happens, we need to pause and take stock.

Sometimes the consensus is innocuous: Yes, incentives do matter. Sometimes it may be appropriately circumscribed, geographically or historically:* Yes, the Soviet economic system

---

* Roger Gordon and Gordon B. Dahl report "broad consensus" among a panel of economists from leading academic departments on fairly specific questions, such as whether "the Fed's new policies in 2011 will increase GDP growth by at least 1% in 2012." They also find, appropriately, that there is greater agreement when the academic literature relevant to the question is large. Gordon and Dahl, "Views among Economists: Professional Consensus or Point-Counterpoint?" *American Economic Review: Papers & Proceedings* 103, no. 3 (2013): 629–35.

was hugely inefficient. At other times, consensus reflects an evaluation after the fact based on accumulated evidence: Yes, the Obama fiscal stimulus of 2009 reduced unemployment. But when a consensus forms around the universal applicability of a conclusion from a specific model, the critical assumptions of which are likely to be violated in many settings—as with perfect competition, say, or full consumer information—we have a problem.

When economists confuse a model for *the* model, two kinds of mischief may follow. First there are the errors of omission, in which a blind spot shows up in the inability to see troubles looming ahead. Most economists, for instance, failed to grasp the dangerous confluence of circumstances that produced the global financial crisis of 2007–8. Then there are the errors of commission, in which fixation on a particular view of the world makes economists complicit in policies whose failure might have been predicted ahead of time. Economists' advocacy of the so-called Washington Consensus and of financial globalization are in this category. Let's consider both types of errors in more depth.

Errors of Omission: The Financial Crisis

Soon after the financial crisis broke, University of Chicago legal theorist and economist Richard Posner castigated his economist colleagues. The profession's leading economists, he wrote, thought another depression was out of the question, asset bubbles never happened, global banks were safe and sound, and the US national debt was nothing to worry about.[4] Yet all these beliefs turned out to be false. The housing bubble burst in 2008, bringing down the US financial industry alongside it and triggering a major government bailout to stabilize the sector. The crisis simultaneously spilled over to Europe and the rest of the world, producing the worst economic downturn since the Great Depression. Unemployment peaked at 10 percent in the United States in October 2009, before coming down to 5.6 percent by the end of 2014. As I write these words in late 2014, nearly one young worker out of four remains unemployed in the countries that are part of the Eurozone.

Many economists were worried about the state of the US economy prior to the crisis. But the main objects of concern were the country's low saving rate and the outsized current account deficit—the large excess of imports over exports. When scenarios of a so-called hard landing were entertained, the focus was a possible sharp depreciation of the US dollar, which would have rekindled inflation and undermined confidence in the US economy. The crisis hit instead in an area where very few people expected it. The soft underbelly of the US economy turned out to be housing and the bloated financial sector that had supercharged it.

A poorly regulated shadow banking sector had created an alphabet soup of new financial instruments. These new derivatives were supposed to have distributed risk to those who were willing to bear it. Instead, they facilitated risk taking and overuse of leverage. They also connected disparate segments of the economy in ways that no one fully grasped at the time, ensuring that failure at one end would precipitate collapse at the other. With a few, but notable, exceptions, such as the future Nobel Prize winner Robert Shiller and the future governor of India's Central Bank and Chicago economist Raghu Rajan, economists overlooked the extent of problems in housing and finance. Shiller had long argued that asset prices were excessively volatile and had focused on a bubble in housing prices.[5] Rajan had fretted about the downside of what was then praised as "financial innovation" and warned as early as 2005 that bankers were taking excessive risks, earning a rebuke from Larry Summers, then president of Harvard, as a "Luddite."[6]

That economists were mostly blind-sided by the crisis is undeniable. Many interpreted this as evidence of a fundamental breakdown in economics. The discipline needed to be rethought and reconfigured. But what makes this episode particularly curious is that there were, in fact, plenty of models to help explain what had been going on under the economy's hood.

Bubbles—steady increases in asset prices divorced from their underlying value—are not a new phenomenon. Their presence was known going back at least to the tulip craze of the seventeenth century and the South Sea bubble of the early eighteenth century. They were the object of study in models of varying complexity, including models based on perfectly rational, forward-looking investors (so-called rational bubbles). The financial crisis of 2008 had all the features of a bank run, and that, too, was a staple of economics. Models of self-fulfilling panic—a coordination failure in which individually rational withdrawals of credit lines produce collective irrationality in the form of a systemic drying up of liquidity—were well known to every student of economics, as were the conditions that facilitate such panics. The need for deposit insurance (coupled with regulation) to prevent bank runs was featured in all finance textbooks.

A key pattern in the run up to the crisis was excessive risk taking by managers of financial institutions. Their compensation depended on it, but their behavior was not consistent with the interests of the banks' shareholders. This divergence between the interests of managers and shareholders is a centerpiece of principal-agent models. These models focus on situations in which a "principal" (a regulator, electorate, or shareholders) tries to control the behavior of an "agent" (a regulated firm, elected government, or CEO) when the latter has more information about the economic environment than the former. The resulting difficulties and inefficiencies should not have come as a surprise to economists. Another incentive distortion centered around credit-rating agencies that evaluated mortgage securities. These agencies were paid by the same financial institutions whose issuances they rated. That they had an incentive to tailor their ratings to the satisfaction of their paymasters ought to have been obvious even to a first-year student in economics.

The economy-wide consequences of asset price collapses

were also familiar to economists after a wave of financial crises experienced by developing countries from the early 1980s on. No one who had studied these episodes should have remained nonchalant about the buildup of private debt in housing and construction in the United States and Europe. The manner in which deleveraging would reverberate throughout the economy, being magnified along the way as banks, firms, and households all tried simultaneously to reduce their debt and build up their financial assets, was also reminiscent of those earlier financial crises.

Clearly, economists did not lack models to understand what was happening. In fact, once the crisis began to play itself out, the models that we just reviewed would prove indispensable for understanding how, for example, China's decision to accumulate large amounts of foreign reserves would ultimately cause a mortgage lender in California to take excessive risks. All the steps in between—the reduction in interest rates as demand for dollar assets went up, the incentive of poorly supervised financial institutions to seek riskier instruments to maintain profits, the building up of financial fragility as portfolios expanded through short-term borrowing, the inability of shareholders to properly rein in bank CEOs, the bubble in housing prices—could be readily explained by existing frameworks. But economists had placed excessive faith in some models at the expense of others, and that turned out to be a big problem.

Many of the favored models revolved around the "efficient-markets hypothesis" (EMH).[7] The hypothesis had been formulated by Eugene Fama, a Chicago finance professor who would subsequently receive the Nobel Prize, somewhat awkwardly, in the same year as Robert Shiller. It says, in brief, that market prices reflect all information available to traders. For an individual investor, the EMH means that, without access to inside information, beating the market repeatedly is impossible. For central bankers and financial regulators, the EMH cautions against trying to move the market in one direction or another. Since all the relevant information is already contained in market prices, any intervention is more likely to distort the market than to correct it.

The EMH does not imply that observers could have foreseen the financial crisis. In fact, since it says changes in asset prices are unpredictable, it implies quite the opposite—that the crisis could *not* have been predicted. Nevertheless, it is hard to square the model with the reality: a sustained rise in asset prices followed by a sharp collapse. To explain it without jettisoning EMH requires us to believe that the financial collapse was caused by a huge rush of "bad news" about the future prospects of the economy, which markets then priced in instantaneously. (This is more or less what Fama himself would argue in 2013.)*

---

* Fama concedes that he doesn't have a reason for why future economic prospects would have worsened so drastically, but he adds that he isn't a macroeconomist, and macroeconomics has never been good at discerning when recessions are coming on. John Cassidy, "Interview with Eugene Fama," *New Yorker*, January 13, 2010, http://www.newyorker.com/news/john-cassidy/interview-with-eugene-fama.

This conclusion reverses the generally accepted line of causation, which goes from the financial crash to the great recession.

Excessive reliance on EMH, to the neglect of models of bubbles and other financial-market pathologies, betrayed a broader set of predilections. There was great faith in what financial markets could achieve. Markets became, in effect, the engine of social progress. They would not only mediate efficiently between savers and investors; they would also distribute risk to those most able to bear it and provide access to credit for previously excluded households, such as those with limited means or no credit history. Through financial innovation, portfolio holders could eke out the maximum return while taking on the least amount of risk.

Moreover, markets came to be viewed not only as inherently efficient and stable, but also as self-disciplining. If big banks and speculators engaged in shenanigans, markets would discover and punish them. Investors who made bad decisions and took inappropriate risks would be driven out; those who behaved responsibly would profit from their prudence. Federal Reserve Chairman Alan Greenspan's *mea culpa* before a 2008 congressional panel would speak volumes about the prevailing state of mind: "Those of us who have looked to the self-interest of lending institutions to protect shareholders' equity, myself included," he confessed, "are in a state of shocked disbelief."[8]

Government, meanwhile, could not be trusted. Bureaucrats and regulators were either captive to special interests or incompetent—and sometimes both at once. The less they did, the better. And in any case, financial markets were now so sophisticated that any effort at regulating them was futile. Financial institutions would always find a way around the regulations. Government was condemned to follow one step behind. Such thinking by economists had legitimized and enabled a great wave of financial deregulation that set the stage for the crisis. And it didn't hurt that these views were shared by some of the top economists in government, such as Larry Summers and Alan Greenspan.

In sum, economists (and those who listened to them) became overconfident in their preferred models of the moment: markets are efficient, financial innovation improves the risk-return trade-off, self-regulation works best, and government intervention is ineffective and harmful. They forgot about the other models. There was too much Fama, too little Shiller. The economics of the profession may have been fine, but evidently there was trouble with its psychology and sociology.

Errors of Commission: The Washington Consensus

In 1989, John Williamson convened a conference in Washington, DC, for major economic policy makers from Latin America. Williamson, an economist at the Institute for International Economics, a Washington think tank (now called the Peterson Institute), was a longtime observer of the region's economies. He had noticed a remarkable convergence of views among policy makers on recommended reforms for Latin America. Virtually identical slates of ideas emanated from international financial institutions such as the World Bank and the International Monetary Fund, think tanks, and various economic agencies of the US government. Economists with PhDs from US universities had meanwhile taken important positions in Latin American governments, and they were rapidly implementing those same policies. In the paper he wrote for the conference, Williamson termed this reform agenda the "Washington Consensus."[9]

The term took off—and took on a life of its own. It came to denote an ambitious agenda that, critics charged, aimed to turn developing nations into textbook cases of free-market economies. This may have been hyperbole, but it accurately described the general drift. The agenda reflected an urge to unshackle these economies from the restraints of government regulation. The policy economists in Latin America and their advisers in Washington were convinced that government intervention had crushed growth and brought about the debt crisis of the 1980s. The remedy could be summarized in three words: "stabilize, privatize, and liberalize." Williamson would frequently protest that his own list had described modest reforms that fell far short of "market fundamentalism," the blanket term for the view that markets are the solution to all public policy problems. But the term "Washington Consensus" fit the zeitgeist of the era only too well.

Advocates of the Washington Consensus—whether in its

original or expanded versions—presented it as good economics. For them, the policies reflected what sound economics teaches: Free markets and competition enable the efficient allocation of scarce resources. Government regulations, trade restrictions, and state ownership create waste and hamper economic growth. But this was an economics that did not go beyond Econ 101, as the advocates ought to have recognized.

One problem was that the Washington Consensus skated over the deeper institutional underpinnings of a market economy, without which none of the market-oriented reforms could reliably deliver their intended benefits. To take the simplest example, in the absence of the rule of law, contract enforcement, and proper antitrust regulations, privatization is as likely to create monopolies for government cronies as it is to foster competition and efficiency. As the importance of institutions sank in, because of the poor response of many economies to Washington Consensus policies, reform efforts expanded in their direction. But it is one thing to slash import tariffs or remove ceilings on interest rates—two common enough approaches—and quite another to install, on short order, institutions that advanced economies acquired over decades, if not centuries. A useful reform agenda had to work with existing institutions, not engage in wishful thinking.

Further still, the Washington Consensus presented a universal recipe. It presumed that all developing countries were pretty much alike—suffering from similar syndromes and in need of an undifferentiated list of reforms. Local context received little consideration, as did the need to prioritize according to urgency or feasibility of reforms. As country after country failed to respond to the reforms, the advocates' instinct was to expand the "to do" list rather than to fine-tune the reforms already in place. So the initial Washington Consensus was supplemented by a burgeoning list of additional measures encompassing labor markets, financial standards, governance improvements, central banking rules, and so on.[10]

The economists behind the Washington Consensus forgot they were operating in an inherently second-best world. As discussed in Chapter 2, in environments where markets are subject to multiple imperfections, the usual intuition on the effects of policies can be quite misleading. Privatization, deregulation, and trade liberalization can all backfire. Market restrictions of a certain sort can be desirable. Policy reforms in these environments require models that explicitly take such second-best complications into account.

Consider how opening up to trade—one of the key items of the Washington Consensus—was supposed to work. As barriers to imports were slashed, firms that were unable to compete internationally would shrink or close down, releasing their resources (workers, capital, managers) to be employed in other parts of the economy. More efficient, internationally competitive sectors, meanwhile, would expand, absorbing those resources and setting the stage for more rapid economic growth. In Latin American and African countries that adopted this strategy, the first part of this prediction largely materialized, but not the second. Manufacturing firms, previously protected by import barriers, took a big hit. But the expansion of new, export-oriented activities based on modern technologies lagged. Workers flooded less productive, informal service sectors such as petty trading instead. Overall productivity suffered.

Why did this happen? Many of the affected markets did not work as expected. Labor markets were not flexible enough to reallocate labor quickly to new, more efficient sectors. Capital markets failed to support the creation of export-oriented firms. The currency remained overvalued, rendering the bulk of manufacturing globally uncompetitive. Coordination failures, knowledge spillovers, and the high cost of establishing a beachhead kept potential entrants out of new areas of comparative advantage. And governments, strapped for cash, were unable to invest in the infrastructure or other forms of support required by nascent industries.

Washington Consensus outcomes in Latin America and Africa stand in sharp contrast with the experience of Asian countries. The latter pursued strategies of global engagement that were explicitly second best. Instead of liberalizing imports early on, South Korea, Taiwan, and later China all began their export push by directly subsidizing homegrown manufacturing. Inefficient manufacturing enterprises were protected during the early stages, to prevent large job losses that would, in all likelihood, lead to the expansion of even less productive informal occupations such as retail trade. These countries also employed macroeconomic and financial controls that kept their currencies competitive in world markets. All of them undertook industrial policies to nurture new manufacturing sectors and reduce their economies' dependence on natural resources. And each country fine-tuned the specifics of its strategy beyond these generalities.

Many observers of Asia's experience and the success of its "unorthodox" policies conclude that these cases have proved standard economics wrong. This interpretation is incorrect. It is true that many of Asia's economic policies do not make sense in light of economic models with well-functioning markets. But these are evidently the wrong models to use. There is very little in China's or South Korea's strategy that cannot be explained by models that take on board some of the major second-best challenges these economies faced.[11] When economists confront the way markets really work—or fail to work—in low-income settings with few firms, high barriers to entry, poor information, and malfunctioning institutions, these alternative models prove indispensable.

Where economists pushed the logic of the Washington Consensus the furthest, with probably the greatest damage, was in financial globalization. Williamson's original list did not include freeing up cross-border capital flow; he was a skeptic about the benefits of financial globalization. Yet by the mid-1990s, removing obstacles to the free flow of capital around the world had become the last frontier of market-based economics. The Organisation for Economic Co-operation and Development (OECD), the rich-country club, made the freeing up of capital movements across countries a precondition for membership. And senior economists at the International Monetary Fund (IMF) tried to enshrine the principle of free capital flow in the organization's charter.

Behind this push lay the thinking of distinguished economists such as onetime MIT professor Stanley Fischer. Fischer had joined the IMF in 1994 as the deputy to its managing director and chief economist. He was well aware that liberalizing financial flow across national borders could create instability. The historical record of free finance certainly presented plenty to worry about. The financial excesses under a previous era of financial globalization during the interwar period—the recurring financial panics and crashes, the painful economic adjustments that flowed from sudden movements in market sentiment, and the tight constraints placed on managing the ups and downs of the macroeconomy—had been foremost on Keynes's mind when he argued for capital controls at the end of the Second World War.

Fischer did not overlook these risks, but he thought they were worth taking. Free capital movement would enable greater efficiency in the global allocation of savings. Capital would flow from where it was plentiful to where it was scarce, thus increasing economic growth. Residents of poor nations would have access both to a larger pool of investible resources and to foreign capital markets to diversify their portfolios. The risks of instability, meanwhile, could be reduced by improving macroeconomic management and enhancing financial regulation.[12] Fischer acknowledged the scant systematic evidence for developing countries benefiting from greater freedom of capital mobility, but he thought it was only a matter of time before such evidence would accrue.

Fischer's implicit model once again significantly discounted second-best complications. He presumed that domestic macroeconomic and regulatory weaknesses could be overcome with sufficient will on the part of governments. In reality, these changes proved much harder to accomplish, in part because economists turned out to know little about what needed to be done. Free capital mobility, coupled with domestic macroeconomic and financial distortions, turned out to have severe adverse outcomes. Access to foreign capital markets allowed domestic banks to binge on short-term foreign debt, and it enabled imprudent governments to borrow more than they ever could on domestic markets. The consequence was a string of painful financial crises in Thailand, South Korea, Indonesia, Mexico, Russia, Argentina, Brazil, Turkey, and elsewhere. The IMF would eventually concede that full liberalization of capital flow was not an appropriate objective for all countries.[13]

There was another problem. Advocates of financial globalization bought into a growth model in which the main driver was the supply of saving and investable funds. In this model, greater access to foreign finance would boost domestic investment and produce higher rates of economic growth. Yet neither investment nor growth rose in the developing countries that opened themselves up to foreign finance. The lack of a positive trend in investment or growth suggested that the constraints to growth in many of these countries lay elsewhere. Firms failed to invest not because they were shut out of finance, but because (for a variety of reasons) they did not foresee high returns. Increased financial flow stimulated consumption rather than investment. Moreover, by appreciating the domestic currency, capital inflow made things worse, by further cutting into the profitability of tradable industries. In this alternative model, apparently describing reality better for many developing and emerging market economies, free capital flow was a poisoned gift.

The good news is that most economists learned their lesson from this experience. On both the Washington Consensus and financial globalization, there is now broad agreement that there had been excessive zeal for a universal approach that oversold the benefits of unfettered markets. Today it is almost a mantra for development economists, finance experts, and international agencies that no single set of policies is appropriate for all countries and that domestic reforms must be tailored to specific circumstances. Common blueprints are out; model selection is in.

The Psychology and Sociology of Economics

Is there something specific to economics that makes its practitioners more likely to commit such errors of omission or commission? Would political scientists and anthropologists, for example, claim a better record for their disciplines in public debates? I am not sure. One difference is that economists are more visible. Because many economists operate in the public sphere and are called upon to advise on policy, their mistakes, when they occur, are more noticeable. Nevertheless, it is worth pondering what makes economists go astray.

To begin with, let's recognize that the public is rarely exposed to the full range of views within economics. The vast majority of economists see themselves as scientists and researchers whose job is to write academic papers, not pontificate on current events or advocate specific policies. These are the kinds of economists who are rarely contacted by journalists or congressional aides, and would likely run away if they were. When they're willing to engage on public issues, they adorn their statements with so many ifs and buts that they have difficulty finding an audience. Most are quintessential ivory-tower economists who would readily grant that they have limited expertise to comment on public matters—at least without further study.

The economists whose voices are heard have either strong convictions, or a willingness to overlook the fine print on policy recommendations. Or both. It is these advocates, with a clear position on the issues, who have a natural advantage in the media, think tanks, and government corridors. Often they are successful "policy entrepreneurs" who make a difference for the better. Auctions of wireless spectrum rights and airline deregulation were both ideas that committed economists convinced politicians to adopt.[14] In other cases, as we've seen, the ideas being trumpeted may be more doubtful, and the advocates' pronouncements may be looked upon with skepticism, or even scorn, by the rest of the profession. But few economist critics will be troubled to challenge them publicly.

At the height of the Washington Consensus craze, I wrote a paper with a graduate student criticizing the unconditional advocacy of freer trade as a growth engine for developing countries.[15] We pointed out that the relationship between trade policy and growth was model- and country-specific. We also showed that there was no strong or uniform evidence one way or another. After circulating and presenting the paper, I got two kinds of reactions. Committed advocates of the Washington Consensus thought I was muddying the waters and undermining the good cause of free trade. But many others expressed their appreciation, complaining that the push for trade liberalization had gone much beyond what economic research was able to support. The second type of reaction was unexpected, since it came from people who had not taken a public stance. They had chosen not to have their voices heard, despite their skepticism. As a result, the public message was not representative of the profession as a whole, where views were, in fact, considerably more hedged.

It is certainly true that economists err on the side of markets. To put it bluntly, economists feel proprietary. They think they understand how markets work, and they fear that most of the public doesn't—and they are largely right on both suppositions. They know that markets can fail in myriad ways. But they think the public's concerns are often ill informed, exaggerated, and unjustified, so they are overly protective of markets. Supply and demand, market efficiency, comparative advantage, incentives—these are the crown jewels of the profession that need defending from the ignorant masses. Or so the thinking goes.

Promoting markets in public debates has today become almost a professional obligation. Economists' contributions in public can therefore look radically different from their discussions in the seminar room. Among colleagues, the shortcomings of markets and the ways in which policy intervention can make things better are fair game. Academic reputations are built on new and imaginative demonstrations of market failure. But in public, the tendency is to close ranks and support free markets and free trade.

This dynamic produces what I call the "barbarians are only on one side" syndrome. Those who want restrictions on markets are organized lobbyists, rent-seeking cronies, and their ilk, while those who want freer markets, even when they're wrong, have their hearts in the right place and are therefore much less dangerous. Taking up the cause of the former gives ammunition to the barbarians, while siding with the latter is, at worst, an honest mistake with no huge consequences.

Forced to take a stand, most economists are likely to cast their vote in favor of the more market-oriented alternative. We can see this leaning in the list of things that command significant consensus among economists at the beginning of this chapter.[16] Of the fourteen items on the full list, only one has a decidedly pro-government bent, in favor of fiscal stimulus during a recession.* A few reflect preferences between different types of policy: budgets should be balanced over the business cycle rather than year by year, cash payments are preferable to payments in kind such as free food, and the welfare system should be replaced with a "negative income tax" (a system of progressive taxation in which poor families receive transfers from the government). The vast majority of the recommendations urge more reliance on markets and less government intervention.

Beyond the general bias toward markets, economists are not always good about drawing the links between their models and the world. Because economists go through a similar training and share a common method of analysis, they act very much like a guild. The models themselves may be the product of analysis, reflection, and observation, but practitioners' views about the real world develop much more heuristically, as a by-product of informal conversations and socialization among themselves. This kind of echo chamber easily produces overconfidence—in the received wisdom or the model of the day. Meanwhile, the guild mentality renders the profession insular and immune

---

* Ninety percent of economists reportedly agree with the following proposition: "Fiscal policy (for example, tax cut and/or government expenditure increase) has a significant stimulative impact on a less than fully employed economy." Greg Mankiw, "News Flash: Economists Agree," February 14, 2009, *Greg Mankiw's Blog*, http://gregmankiw .blogspot.com/2009/02/news-flash-economists-agree.html.

to outside criticism. The models may have problems, but only card-carrying members of the profession are allowed to say so. The objections of outsiders are discounted because they do not understand the models. The profession values smarts over judgment, being interesting over being right—so its fads and fashions do not always self-correct.

These problems are compounded by the fact that accepted practice does not require economists to think through the conditions under which their models are useful. Asked point-blank, they can state chapter and verse all the assumptions needed to generate a particular result; that is, after all, the point of modeling. But ask them whether the model is more relevant to Bolivia or to Thailand, or whether it resembles more the market for cable TV or the market for oranges, and they will have a hard time producing an articulate answer. The standards of the profession require that the modeler make only some general claims about how what he or she is doing is relevant to the real world. It is left to the reader or the user of the model to infer the specific circumstances in which the model can help us better understand reality.* This fudge factor increases the chances of malpractice. Models lifted out of their original context can be used in settings for which they are inappropriate.

---

* As University of East Anglia economist Robert Sugden points out, "In economics . . . there seems to be a convention that modellers need not be explicit about what their models tell us about the real world." Sugden, "Credible Worlds, Capacities and Mechanisms" (unpublished paper, School of Economics, University of East Anglia, August 2008), 18.

At the empirical end of economics, such as labor and development economics, where almost all economists work directly with data and real-world evidence, paradoxically the problems may be even more severe. This is because the underlying model is often left unspecified from the outset. The empirical nature of the analysis may make us think that we've learned more than we have. Many empirical researchers believe that their work does not require models at all. After all, they are simply asking whether something works or whether A causes B. But behind all causal assertions lie a model of some sort. If greater education results in higher earnings, for example, is that because of the returns to education or because education provides incentives to work harder, thereby also increasing earnings?[17] Being explicit about those models clarifies the nature of the finding and also highlights their contingent character. Once the model is laid out, we can see what the finding depends on and how easily the finding can be extrapolated to other settings.

As we've seen, some of the most interesting applied work these days takes the form of randomized field experiments in which the researcher tests whether specific policy interventions produce the intended effects (or not). These are meant to speak directly to how the real world works—in one particular setting. But they again remain largely silent about the specific conditions under which the findings apply—the features of the economy and society to which the intervention may have been particularly suited—and those under which we shouldn't expect them to apply. They can easily produce the impression that the results are general when they are, in fact, deeply context-specific.

The bottom line is that there is much to complain about in the practices and professional biases of economists. But are these shortcomings fundamental problems that render the entire discipline an inherently flawed approach to social reality? I do not think so.

Power and Responsibility

Why do economists wield power beyond the classroom in the first place? It is not evident that they should, given that most of the discipline's practitioners are content with producing research articles for each other and crave no such power.

The twin origins of their supposed power are slightly in tension with each other. First, their discipline has scientific pretensions; it brings useful knowledge to bear on public policy questions. Second, their models provide narratives that lodge easily in the popular consciousness. These fable-like narratives often have morals that can be formulated in catchy terms (for example, "taxation kills incentives") and also sync up with clear political ideologies. The science and the storytelling parts are usually complementary, as I explained in Chapter 1. Working in tandem, they enable economists' beliefs to gain tremendous traction in the public debate.

Mischief occurs when economists begin to treat a model as *the* model. Then the narrative takes on a life of its own and becomes dislodged from the setting that produced it. It turns into an all-purpose explanation that obscures alternative, and potentially more useful, story lines. Luckily, the antidote exists—within economics. The corrective is for economists to return to the seminar room and remind themselves of the other models in their collection.

In an earlier book, I wrote that there are two kinds of economists, drawing on a distinction made famous by the British philosopher Isaiah Berlin. Even though I had in mind specialists on the international economy at the time, the idea applies more broadly.[18] "Hedgehogs" are captivated by a single big idea—markets work best, governments are corrupt, intervention backfires—which they apply unremittingly. "Foxes," by contrast, lack a grand vision and hold many different views about the world—some of them contradictory. The hedgehog's take on a problem can always be predicted: the solution lies in freer markets, regardless of the exact nature of and context for the economic problem. Foxes will answer, "It depends"; sometimes they recommend more markets, sometimes more government.

Economics needs fewer hedgehogs and more foxes engaged in public debates. Economists who are able to navigate from one explanatory framework to another as circumstances require are more likely to point us in the right direction.

CHAPTER 6

Economics and Its Critics

A n economist, a physician, and an architect are travel-
ing on a train together, and they fall into a discussion as to which one of their professions is the most
honorable. The physician points out that God created Eve out
of Adam's rib, so He must have been a surgeon. The architect
jumps in and says, "Before Adam and Eve existed, the universe
had to be created out of chaos, and that surely was a feat of
architecture." At which point, the economist says, "And where
do you think chaos came from?"*

Economics without its critics would be like Hamlet without
the prince. The discipline's scientific pretensions, its exalted
status within the social sciences, and its practitioners' influence

---

* I heard this joke on a BBC radio program when I was a college student,
and it was told, characteristically, by an economist, E. F. Schumacher.
Economists are their own harshest critics.

in public debates are a magnet for detractors. Critics accuse economists of having a reductionist approach to social phenomena, making unfounded universal claims, ignoring the social, cultural, and political context, reifying markets and material incentives, and having a conservative bias. I have complained myself at length in this book about two weaknesses: the lack of attention to model selection and the excessive focus at times on some models at the expense of others. In plenty of instances economists have led the world astray.

But I will argue in this chapter that much of the broader criticism misses its mark. Economics is a collection of models that admits a wide diversity of possibilities, rather than a set of prepackaged conclusions. As three economists, themselves critics, put it, standard accounts "tend to miss the diversity that exists within the profession, and the many new ideas that are being tried out," and they often overlook the reality that "one can be part of the mainstream and yet not necessarily hold 'orthodox' ideas."[1] The critics do have a point when they say economists act in ways that suggest otherwise, by preaching universal solutions or market fundamentalism. But critics also need to understand that economists who do this are, in fact, not being true to their own discipline. Such economists deserve their fellow economists' rebuke as much as outsiders' reproach. Once this point is recognized, many of the standard criticisms are nullified or lose their bite.

Reconsidering the Usual Criticisms

We have seen some of the leading criticisms under various guises in earlier chapters,. Take the complaint that economic models are too simple. This objection misunderstands the nature of analysis. Simplicity is, in fact, a requirement of science. Every explanation, hypothesis, causal account is necessarily an idealization; it leaves many things out so that it can focus on the essence. The term "analysis" itself has its roots in Greek, where it signifies the breaking of complex things into simpler elements. It is the antonym of "synthesis," which refers to combining things. Neither analysis nor synthesis is possible without these simpler components.

Simple need not mean simplistic, of course. As Einstein is supposed to have said, "Everything should be made as simple as possible, but no simpler." When causal mechanisms interact strongly with each other and cannot be studied in isolation, models do need to include those interactions. If a coffee blight, say, both raises costs of production and disrupts a price-fixing agreement among principal coffee exporters, we cannot analyze the effects of each—the supply shock and the reduced cartelization—separately. Such models will be more complicated than others. But they will still fall far short of claiming to represent social reality in any great detail. If this is what the advocates of complexity have in mind, there can be no objection to it. When, on the other hand, the underlying relationships remain nebulous or undefined, and purported explanations do not build on such simple elements, complexity can only lead to incoherence.

So, too, consider the related criticism that economic models make unrealistic assumptions. Economics stands guilty as charged. Many assumptions that go into economic models—perfect competition, perfect information, perfect foresight—are patently untrue. But as I explained in Chapter 1, models with unrealistic assumptions can be as useful as lab experiments performed under conditions that depart starkly from the real world. Both allow us to identify a cause-effect relationship by isolating it from other confounding factors. Critical assumptions—those that relate directly to the substantive result or the question asked—are where care is required. We would not want to build an airplane on principles that derive from a vacuum.

Consider the effects of a sales tax on cars. The degree to which consumers think of small and large cars as the same (as substitutes for each other) is not of great interest when we contemplate the effects of a (percentage) tax on all cars across the board. We might as well assume that these types of cars are perfect substitutes. But if the tax is on luxury cars alone, the perfect-substitutes assumption is no longer innocuous. The effects on government revenue and car sales will depend critically on the size of what economists call the cross-price elasticity of demand (the sensitivity of demand for one category of goods to the price of another category). The larger this elasticity (in absolute value), the greater the shift in con-sumer purchases from large to small cars, and the lower the tax revenues collected by the government. Economists have to ensure that their prescriptions hold even when assumptions become more realistic.

Since they take the individual as their unit of analysis, econ-omists are frequently criticized for neglecting the role of social and cultural determinants of behavior. Sociologists and anthro-pologists often seek explanation for outcomes at the level of the community or society instead of individuals. (Economists' preference for basing aggregate outcomes on individual deci-sions is called "methodological individualism" and is similar to the proclivity toward microfoundations in macroeconomics.) Cultural practices and social norms are what valorize certain categories of consumption and behavior and stigmatize oth-ers, these critics argue, and they often play the determining role even when economic decisions such as consumption and employment are involved. Economists' obsession with choices made by individual households or investors, according to this line of thought, obscures the fact that preferences and behav-ioral patterns are "socially constructed," or imposed by the structure of society.[2]

It is certainly true that economists' most basic benchmark models neglect the social and cultural roots of people's prefer-ences and constraints. But there is no reason the models can-not be extended to incorporate these influences and to work out their implications. In fact, an active research program in economics does exactly this, analyzing how identities, norms, and cultural practices are shaped by the interaction of individuals with each other.[3] Unless one believes that humans have no agency at all, that their behavior is fully determined by external forces outside their control, any reasonable explanation of social phenomena must square these phenomena with the actions that individuals *choose* to take. Economists' models, based as they are on explicit consideration of the constraints (material, social, contextual) under which these decisions are made, are well equipped for this kind of analysis. From the perspective of good social analysis, the contrast between individual- and societal-level analyses sets up a largely false and unhelpful dichotomy.

Do economists have a bias toward market-based solutions? Again, probably guilty as charged. As I've already shown, however, here the problem has to do more with the way economists present themselves in public than with the substance of the discipline. Research careers these days are made not by demonstrating how markets work, but by generating interesting counterexamples to Adam Smith's Invisible Hand dictum. It may surprise the reader, for example, that the most vociferous advocate of free trade in the profession, Jagdish Bhagwati, owes his academic reputation to a series of models that showed how free trade could leave a nation worse off.* The solution to the

---

* Jagdish Bhagwati has been a tireless advocate of free trade since the 1980s. In his early academic work, he showed that an open economy may

bias is not to remake economics, but to better reflect the diversity of models that already exists in the public debate.

Then there is the criticism that economists' theories cannot be properly tested. Empirical analysis is never conclusive, and invalid theories are rarely rejected. The discipline hobbles from one set of preferred models to another, driven less by evidence than by fads and ideology. Insofar as economists present themselves as the physicists of the social world, this criticism is deserved. As I explained earlier, however, comparisons to natural sciences are misleading. Economics is a *social* science, which means that the search for universal theories and results is futile. A model (or theory) is at best contextually valid. Expecting general empirical validation or rejection makes little sense.

Economics advances by expanding the collection of potentially applicable models, with newer ones capturing aspects of social reality that were overlooked or neglected by earlier ones. When an economist encounters a new pattern, his reaction is to think of a model that might explain it. Economics advances also by better methods of model selection—

---

lose something from growth, because of attendant changes in the world prices of its imports and exports. He also analyzed at length the presence of market distortions and the needed policy responses, showing that laissez-faire was suboptimal under a wide range of conditions. Jagdish Bhagwati, "Immiserizing Growth: A Geometrical Note," *Review of Economic Studies* 25, no. 3 (June 1958): 201–5; Bhagwati and V. K. Ramaswami, "Domestic Distortions, Tariffs and the Theory of Optimum Subsidy," *Journal of Political Economy* 71, no. 1 (February 1963): 44–50.

improving the match between model and real-world setting. As I explained in Chapter 3, this is more a craft than a science, and one that does not get the attention it deserves in economics. But the advantage of working with models is that the elements required for model selection—the critical assumptions, the causal channels, the direct and indirect implications—are all transparent and laid bare. These elements enable economists to check the correspondence between the model and the setting, informally and suggestively, even if not formally and conclusively.

Finally, economics is faulted for its failure to predict. God created economic forecasters to make astrologers look good, quipped John Kenneth Galbraith (himself an economist). Exhibit A in recent times has been the global financial crisis, which unfolded at a time when the vast majority of economists had been lulled into thinking macroeconomic and financial stability had arrived for good. I explained in the previous chapter that this misperception was another by-product of the usual blind spot: mistaking a model for *the* model. Paradoxically, had economists taken their own models more seriously, they would have been less confident about the consequences of financial innovation and financial globalization and more prepared for the financial whiplash that resulted.

However, no social science should claim to make predictions and be judged on that basis. The direction of social life cannot be predicted. There are too many drivers at work. To put it in the language of models, there are numerous models of the future, including those that have yet to be formulated! At best, we can expect economics and other social sciences to make *conditional* predictions: to tell us the likely outcomes of individual changes, taken one at a time, while other factors remain constant. That is what good models do. They can provide a guide to the consequences of certain large-scale changes or to the effects when some causes swamp others. We can be reasonably sure that massive price controls will lead to shortages, that a harvest failure will raise coffee prices, and that a huge injection of money by a central bank will produce inflation in normal times. But in these instances, "everything else remains the same" is a reasonable assumption, and predictions look more like conditional predictions. The trouble is that often we can neither guess which among many plausible changes will actually take place, nor be confident about their relative weights in the ultimate outcome. In such instances, economics demands caution and modesty rather than self-confidence.

In the rest of the chapter, I will take up two other major criticisms that until now I've not said much about. First, I'll discuss the charge that economics is rife with value judgments and that much of what passes as scientific analysis in fact merely expresses a normative preference for a market-based society. Second, I'll evaluate the contention that economics discourages pluralism and is hostile to new approaches and ideas.

The Question of Values

Most models in economics assume that individuals behave self-ishly. They try to maximize their own (and perhaps also their children's) consumption possibilities, and they don't care what happens to others. In many settings this is sufficiently realistic. The polar-opposite assumption of completely selfless behavior would not make sense. And allowing some degree of altruism and generosity would not substantially alter many of the results.

A fair amount of research relaxes this stark assumption and allows for some degree of altruism and other-regarding behavior as well. In some settings—charity or voting in general elections, for example—additional motivations besides self-interest are indispensable for understanding what's going on. Nonetheless, it is fair to say that self-interested behavior forms a benchmark assumption in economics. But the models are meant to describe what *actually* happens, not what should happen. There are no value judgments in this kind of analysis.

The crowning achievement of economics, the Invisible Hand Theorem, perhaps does make economists somewhat more nonchalant and permissive toward displays of self-interest. After all, its key insight is that self-interest can be yoked to public purpose. A collection of selfish people need not produce economic and social chaos. From society's standpoint, the antidote to the pursuit of material advantage by some is the pursuit of material advantage by many others.

Free and unhindered competition neutralizes pathologies that might otherwise have arisen.

There is an apt parallel here with the constitutional design of the United States. James Madison, Alexander Hamilton, and the others who were behind the US federal system took it as a given that a political system would operate around the self-interest of organized pressure groups. They designed the system accordingly, with checks and balances. The multiplicity of centers of power and the restraints placed on their authority, along with the sheer scale of the union, would prevent any one faction from gaining the upper hand. It would be unfair to criticize the Federalists for having enshrined self-interest in US politics; they thought they were simply dealing with its consequences. Similarly, economists whose models are populated by selfish consumers are not taking a moral stand; they're only describing what happens when such consumers interact with equally self-interested firms in the marketplace.

But does this benchmark role of self-interest in economic models produce a normative bias in its favor? We can ask whether it "normalizes" such behavior (makes it the norm) and crowds out other, more socially oriented behavior. A finding that appears to amplify this concern is that college students who major in economics tend to act in more self-interested ways than do those who major in other fields. Their behavior is more consistent with benchmark economic models such as the prisoners' dilemma. Some have interpreted this result as evidence that studying economics makes individuals more selfish.

In fact, the results point in the direction of an alternative hypothesis: certain types of students are more likely than others to go into economics. Research on Israeli students has found that differences in values between economics students and noneconomics students were already in place before the former group enrolled in their economics course of study. Research from Switzerland shows that while certain types of prospective economics majors (those focusing on business) start their college career with a lower propensity to donate funds for needy students, this propensity does not decline with the study of economics.[4] So it may be true that economics attracts different kinds of students—more selfish ones! But evidence for the charge that it somehow renders people more selfish is weaker.

Because self-interest features prominently in economic models, economists exhibit a bias toward incentive-based solutions to public problems. Consider climate change and the question of how to address carbon emissions. Public opinion varies greatly, but economists are virtually unanimous: they recommend either taxing carbon or implementing a close equivalent, a quota on carbon emissions with trading of emission allowances.* In both cases the aim is to make it

---

* These two policies are totally equivalent in a complete-information world, but they produce different outcomes under uncertainty.

more expensive and hence less profitable for firms to use carbon. To economists, the policy is the correct one because it acts on the relevant margin. Firms fail to take into account the environmental effects of their decisions, so the right response is to force them to "internalize" the external costs by paying for carbon.

This remedy does not sit well with many noneconomists. It appears to turn a moral responsibility—"thou shalt not despoil the environment"—into a cost-benefit calculus. Going further, some would say that a carbon tax or emission trading legitimizes pollution. The message to firms seems to be that emitting carbon and contributing to climate change is OK as long as you pay a fee. The Harvard political philosopher Michael Sandel has been a vocal critic in recent years of what he thinks is economics' harmful effects on public culture. Here is Sandel on material incentives:

> Putting a price on the good things in life can corrupt them. That's because markets don't only allocate goods; they express and promote certain attitudes toward the goods being exchanged. Paying kids to read books might get them to read more, but might also teach them to regard reading as a chore rather than a source of intrinsic satisfaction. Hiring foreign mercenaries to fight our wars might spare the lives of our citizens, but might also corrupt the meaning of citizenship.[5]

In other words, reliance on markets and incentives fosters values that are corrosive and undermine social objectives.

An economist might respond that they look at objectives like emission control not as moral matters, but as questions of effectiveness. Moral exhortation is fine, but incentives work. If they get more pushback, economists are likely to appeal to empiricism. Fine, they will say, we can show you hundreds of studies indicating that firms reduce their use of, say, oil when its price goes up; show us the evidence that moral exhortation achieves a reduction in carbon emissions.

Economists' instinct is to take the world, including human selfishness, as given and to engineer solutions around that perceived constraint. They would argue, correctly, that this has nothing to do with their values and ethics, but with their empirical orientation. If this makes them sometimes too quick to pooh-pooh non-incentive-based solutions, it also makes them willing to acknowledge when evidence comes in that suggests their opponents have a point.

I mentioned in passing in Chapter 2 an unexpected real-life experiment that caused quite a stir among economists. To reduce tardiness, an Israeli day care had instituted a penalty for parents who showed up late to pick up their children. This policy was in line with what economists would have recommended: if you want to reduce a behavior, make it more costly for the individuals who exhibit the behavior. To virtually everyone's surprise, tardiness actually increased after the penalty was put in place. Apparently, now that there was a fee, parents felt it was OK to show up late. A moral injunction that previously had kept parents' behavior in check was relaxed once the monetary penalty came into play. Or to put it in economists' terms, the moral cost of tardiness was reduced, and perhaps eliminated. As the economist Sam Bowles points out, this is an example of how material incentives may sometimes crowd out moral, or other-regarding behavior.[6]

The lesson for economists is that sometimes they need a richer paradigm of human behavior (or of costs and benefits) than they use in the simplest models. Economists are usually willing to think in those terms and to make the required modifications, as long as there is evidence suggesting that the benchmark model fails. It clearly did in this case. But they would continue to regard this extension not in moral terms, but in terms of relevance and efficacy. For example, does the lesson of the Israeli day care speak also to carbon control? Is it realistic to think that power plants operate in a moral universe regarding the climate-change imperative that will be substantially affected by the imposition of a carbon tax? Are public education campaigns, consciousness raising, or moral exhortation likely to have a greater impact on carbon emissions? To economists, these are empirical and not moral questions.

What about Sandel's broader charge that markets breed "market values," that they make us exchange things on markets that shouldn't be? "We live in a time," Sandel writes, "when almost everything can be bought and sold." Everything, in his words, "is up for sale." Here are some of the examples that Sandel cites in addition to carbon emission fees: a prison cell upgrade for $90 a night in Santa Ana; access to the carpool lane for a car with a single rider for $8 in Minneapolis and other cities; an Indian surrogate mother for $8,000; the right to shoot an endangered black rhino for $250,000; a doctor's cell phone number for $1,500.[7] These and other examples illustrate for Sandel the increasing role that market values play in our social life.

But what are these market values? Deep down there is really only one: efficiency. All that an economist can claim about a market—and one that works well, without the frequent imperfections—is that it yields an efficient allocation of resources in a precise sense: there is no feasible way to make some people richer without making others poorer. Any economist who makes a broader argument about the fairness, justice, or moral worth of markets that is based on economics proper is simply engaged in malpractice.

The market-efficiency connection, of course, doesn't preclude individual economists from attaching additional values to markets. For example, an economist's personal values may make him an advocate of free enterprise on account of libertarian beliefs—the view that the liberty to engage in commerce with whomever one likes should not be abridged. But these beliefs originate outside economics. Their advocacy by an economist gives them no greater credence than their espousal by an architect or physician. Nor does it preclude the assertion, based on specific evidence, that less intervention in markets in certain cases may produce benefits beyond efficiency. For example, economists often argue that the removal of fuel subsidies in developing countries would enhance distributional equity alongside efficiency. The reason is that subsidies not only cause overconsumption of fuel (which is the source of their inefficiency), but also benefit mostly the well-to-do (who are the main users of the subsidized fuel). But such arguments have to be demonstrated empirically, on a case-by-case basis.

Is efficiency a good thing? Yes it is, taken on its own. We can say without hesitation that efficiency is a consideration—a value—worth taking into account when we compare alternative social states. But it is certainly not the only one. Equity would be another contending value, as would be the intrinsic moral value of other-regarding and socially responsible behaviors. Sometimes these considerations push us in the same direction as efficiency, and therefore reinforce the case for markets. At other times there may be tensions and trade-offs to consider. What should and should not be sold on markets is ultimately a question decided by evaluating trade-offs in many different dimensions. Different communities are likely to arrive at different answers. And the answers may change over time even within the same community. Once again, the economist has no special expertise in making those trade-offs. At best, economists can provide useful input.

For example, economists may contribute to the discussion of charging solo riders a fee for access to the carpool lane. They can make educated guesses as to the type of rider that is most likely to pay the extra fee; the gains reaped by those who benefit (by arriving at their destination quicker); the funds generated by the turnpike authority and their possible uses; and the distributional incidence of the potential congestion costs in the carpool lane (who pays, and how much?). The evidence on these questions may end up swaying most people to the view that the fee option is, on balance, desirable. The same kind of analysis for, say, a prison cell upgrade may result in the opposite conclusion. In neither case would it be justifiable for economists to advocate the market option as a general solution, without acknowledging the multiple considerations beyond efficiency.

To be fair to Sandel, his is not a straw man argument. Economists do get careless and make claims that are broader than their economist licenses really allow. Remember the list from the previous chapter of things on which the vast majority of economists agree? Many of them involve implicit value judgments. When economists say foreign trade should not be restricted, outsourcing should not be prohibited, or agricultural subsidies should be eliminated, they've rendered judgments on matters that cannot be evaluated solely on grounds of efficiency. Questions of justice, ethics, fairness, and distribution are tangled up in all of them. Is it necessarily fair to push for free trade if the beneficiaries are predominantly wealthy individuals and the losers are some of the poorest workers in our society? Is it fair to reap the benefits of outsourcing from poor countries where workers lack fundamental rights and toil under hazardous workplace conditions? The 90-plus percent of economists who agreed with these statements must either have been unaware of these questions or consistently subsumed them under efficiency considerations. Either way, there is a problem. Even assuming that the efficiency consequences can be readily and universally predicted—and the concerns I raised in the previous chapter can be downplayed—economists are, without doubt, overreaching in these particular areas.

Since their training provides them with no tool to evaluate alternative social states other than the lens of allocative efficiency, economists are prone to make this mistake whenever called upon to comment on public policies. They can easily conflate efficiency with other social goals. A useful rebuttal would call the economists' bluff and remind them of the specific ways in which they're transgressing the boundaries of their expertise. By the same token, economists must remind the public that many claims made by politicians and other policy entrepreneurs on their behalf cannot find full justification in the discipline.

One of the earliest and most influential noneconomic arguments on behalf of markets was that engagement in market activities would moderate human temperament. As Albert Hirschman reminds us in his magisterial book *The Passions and the Interest*, the thinkers of the late seventeenth and eighteenth centuries reasoned that the profit-seeking motive would countervail baser human motivations such as the urge for violence and domination over other men. The term "doux" (meaning "sweet") was often appended to "commerce" to suggest that commercial activities promoted gentle and peaceful interactions. Montesquieu famously said, "Wherever manners are gentle there is commerce; and wherever there is commerce, manners are gentle." Thanks to commerce, pointed out Samuel Ricard, David Ricardo's grandfather, man seeks virtues such as deliberation, honesty, and prudence. He stays away from vice lest he lose his credit and become an object of scandal. In this way, interests could mollify the passions.[8]

These early philosophers encouraged the spread of markets not for reasons of efficiency or for the expansion of material resources, but because they thought it would produce a more ethical, more harmonious society. It is ironic that three centuries later, markets have come to be associated in the eyes of many with moral corruption. Just as today's advocates of markets overlook the limits of efficiency, perhaps the critics neglect some of the ways in which markets contribute to a spirit of cooperation.

Lack of Pluralism

One of the most frequent complaints about economics labels it a club that shuns outsiders. This exclusiveness makes the discipline insular, according to the critics, and closed to new and alternative perspectives on economics. Economics should become more inclusive, they argue, more pluralistic and more welcoming of unorthodox approaches.

This criticism is one that students voice often, partly because of the way economics is taught. In the fall of 2011, for example, a group of students staged a walkout in Harvard's popular introductory economics course, Economics 10, taught by my colleague Greg Mankiw. Their complaint was that the course propagates conservative ideology in the guise of economic science and helps perpetuate social inequality. Mankiw dismissed the protesters as "poorly informed." He pointed out that economics does not have an ideology; it is just a method that enables us to think straight and reach correct answers, with no foreordained policy conclusions.[9]

In April 2014, a student group at Manchester University calling itself the Post-Crash Economics Society put out a sixty-page manifesto advocating substantial reform of economics education. The report included a foreword by Andrew Haldane, a high-ranking official of the Bank of England, and received plaudits from many other economists. It criticized economics teaching for being too narrow and argued for greater pluralism and an infusion of perspectives from ethics, history, and politics. The monopoly of the standard economic paradigm, the students wrote, prevented "meaningful critical thinking" and was therefore harmful to economics on its own terms.*

---

* *Economics, Education and Unlearning: Economics Education at the University of Manchester*, Post-Crash Economics Society (PCES), April 2014, http://www.post-crasheconomics.com/download/778r. The Oxford economist Simon Wren-Lewis has a good discussion of what's right and wrong with the students' criticism in "When Economics Students Rebel," *Mainly Macro* (blog), April 24, 2014, http://mainlymacro.blogspot.co.uk/2014/04/when-economics-students-rebel.html.

How do we understand these complaints in light of the patent multiplicity of models within economics? The trouble from the students' perspective is that much of what goes on in an introductory course in economics is a paean to markets. It gives little sense of the diversity of conclusions in economics, to which the student is unlikely to be exposed unless she goes on to take many more economics courses. Economics professors are charged with being narrow and ideological because they are their own worst enemy when it comes to communicating their discipline to outsiders. Instead of presenting a taste of the full panoply of perspectives that their discipline offers, they focus on benchmark models that stress one set of conclusions. This is particularly so in introductory courses, where the professor is keen to demonstrate how markets work. As the Oxford economist Simon Wren-Lewis points out, "One of the sad things about the way economics is often taught is that students do not see much of the interesting stuff that is going on [in the discipline]."[10] Can one fault students for demanding an alternative perspective?

I myself have frequently flouted conventional wisdom among economists, but with no apparent damage to my career (at least I don't think so!). I may not be sufficiently radical for many noneconomists, but I am often viewed as unorthodox within the discipline. An economist colleague at Harvard would greet me by saying, "How is the revolution going?" every time he saw me. Yet even though I reach policy conclusions that differ from prevailing academic views in many of my writings, I have never really felt discriminated against in the profession. I don't think my research papers have been judged more harshly by journal editors or by my peers because of the inferences they drew.

Pluralism with respect to conclusions is one thing; pluralism with respect to methods is something else. No academic discipline is permissive of approaches that diverge too much from prevailing practices, and economics is unforgiving of those who violate the way work in the discipline is done. An aspiring economist has to formulate clear models and apply appropriate statistical techniques. These models can incorporate a wide range of assumptions; without leeway here, it would be impossible to reach novel or unconventional conclusions. But not all assumptions are equally acceptable. In economics, this means that the greater the departure from benchmark assumptions, the greater the burden of justifying and motivating why those departures are needed.

To be counted as an insider, as someone whose work should be taken seriously, you have to operate within these rules. If my work has been accepted within economics, it is because I've followed the rules. I do so not because the rules enable me to display my credentials, but because I find them useful. The rules have disciplined my research and have ensured that I know what I'm talking about. But they have not been so constraining as to prevent me from pursuing interests or paths of analysis that would produce unorthodox conclusions.

So economics offers limited room for methodological pluralism—much less than it allows for diversity in policy conclusions. Most economists would say this is a good thing, because it provides protection against shoddy thinking and poor empirical data. Some methods are better than others. Formal frameworks that explicitly identify cause-effect links are better than verbal accounts that leave interactions open to diverse interpretations. Models that explain social phenomena by analyzing the behavior of the actors that shape them, as economists do when they talk about market competition, coordination failures, or prisoners' dilemmas, are better than those that ascribe agency to amorphous social movements. Empirical analyses that pay attention to issues of causality and "omitted variable bias" are better than those that do not.

For some, these constraints represent a kind of methodological straitjacket that crowds out new thinking. But it is easy to exaggerate the rigidity of the rules within which the profession operates.* In my own experience, I have seen economics change drastically over a period of three short decades.

Consider the fields that I focused on in graduate school in the

---

* Even relatively sophisticated accounts of the economics profession by outsiders typically overstate the rigidity of the discipline and understate the possibilities of change over time. As an example, see Marion Fourcade, Etienne Ollion, and Yann Algan, *The Superiority of Economists*, MaxPo Discussion Paper 14/3 (Paris: Max Planck Sciences Po Center on Coping with Instability in Market Societies, 2014). The paper emphasizes the homogeneity of the discipline even as it cites many of the changes that have taken place and that I cite below.

mid-1980s. The three in which I wrote exams were economic development, international economics, and industrial organization. All three have undergone a dramatic makeover. Most important, all of them have become predominantly empirical rather than theoretical subjects. At the time I was working on my dissertation, the best and brightest in these fields focused on applied theory, producing mathematical models that attempted to shed light on a particular facet of the economy. Evidence was used to motivate the models, and sometimes to buttress their results. But it was unusual to devote the bulk of the work to empirical analysis. Only the lesser students, the ones without bright ideas and theoretical skills, would attempt empirically testing this or that model.

These days, it is virtually impossible to publish in top journals in two of those fields—development and international economics—without including some serious empirical analysis. And industrial organization has become much more empirical too, though not as empirical as the other two fields. Moreover, what passes as acceptable empirical analysis has changed forever. The standards of the profession now require much greater attention to the quality of the data, to causal inference from evidence, and to a variety of statistical pitfalls. All in all, this empirical turn has been good for the profession. In international economics, for example, empirical work has generated new findings on the importance of quality and productivity differences among firms participating in international trade and an expanded variety of models to account for them. In development economics, new evidence has led to policy innovations in health, education, and finance that have the potential to improve the lives of hundreds of millions of people.

Another way we can observe the transformation of the discipline is by looking at the new areas of research that have flourished in recent decades. Three of these are particularly noteworthy: behavioral economics, randomized controlled trials (RCTs), and institutions. What's striking is that all these areas have been greatly influenced, and in fact stimulated, by fields from outside economics—psychology, medicine, and history, respectively. Their growth disproves the claim that economics is insular and ignores the contributions of other cognate disciplines.

In some ways, the rise of behavioral economics marks the greatest departure for standard economics because it undercuts the benchmark, almost canonical assumption of economic models: that individuals are rational. The rationality postulate not only seems sensible in a lot of settings, but also allows the modeling of behavior by relying on standard mathematical optimization techniques in which individuals maximize (or minimize, as the case may be) well-defined objective functions under budgetary and other constraints. Using these techniques, economists derive specific predictions for how consumers choose which products to buy, how households save, how firms invest, how workers search for jobs, and so on—as well as for how these actions depend on the particulars of the setting.

The postulate always had its critics from within economics, such as Herbert Simon, who argued for a limited form of rationality (called "bounded rationality"), and Richard Nelson, who proposed that firms move by trial and error rather than by optimization—not to mention Adam Smith himself, who may have been the first behavioral economist.[11] But it was the work of psychologist Daniel Kahneman and his coauthors that had the greatest impact on mainstream economics.[12] This contribution was recognized by a Nobel memorial prize in economics given to Kahneman in 2002, the first time that the prize was awarded to a noneconomist.*

Kahneman and his colleagues' experiments cataloged a long list of behavioral regularities that violated rationality, as the concept is used in economics. People value an object more when giving it up than they do when acquiring it (loss aversion), overgeneralize from small amounts of data (overconfidence), discount evidence that contradicts their beliefs (confirmation bias), yield to short-term temptations that they realize are bad for them (weak self-control), value fairness and reciprocity (bounded selfishness), and so on. These types of behavior have important implications in many areas of economics. For example, the efficient-markets hypothesis in finance (see Chapter 5) relies on investors having unbiased expectations. When economists began to introduce these new findings in their models,

---

* In 2009 the prize went to Elinor Ostrom, a political scientist, for her work on institutions and managing common-pool resources.

they were able to account for financial-market anomalies that had long resisted explanation. For example, the apparent over-sensitivity of asset prices to news could be explained by the tendency of people to overreact to recent information.[13] These insights from social psychology were subsequently applied to many areas of decision making, such as saving behavior, choice of medical insurance, and fertilizer use by poor farmers.[14] Behavioral economics moved from the fringes to become one of the liveliest areas of economics, attracting the best talent in the profession.

RCTs are a departure of a different sort. They represent a giant leap in the direction of empiricism. Their goal is to generate clear-cut, unambiguous evidence from the ground up. Empirical work in economics has always been plagued by the difficulty of uncovering true causal relationships. The world never stands still to allow the researcher to cleanly pinpoint how, for example, subsidizing insecticide-treated bed nets affects malaria incidence. Too many other things change along the way, confounding the effect we're looking for. Economists began to study such questions using randomization. So, for example, bed nets could be distributed to a random sample of recipients (the treatment group), with nonrecipients constituting a natural control group. The difference between outcomes for the two groups would then be attributed to the effect of the intervention. This approach was relatively simple, compared to complex statistical techniques. It was also quite effective in identifying what works and what doesn't in a particular setting. Generalizing from one set of results remained, as usual, more problematic, because it required extrapolating to different conditions.

Poor countries presented particularly suitable conditions for carrying out such experiments in the field. There was extensive debate about which kinds of remedies would work best in those settings, and there was room to try out different interventions. The gains from identifying effective interventions were huge, given the prevailing levels of poverty. Some aspects of RCTs remain controversial. Critics have complained that RCT advocates make exaggerated claims about how much we can learn from field experiments studying the nature of underdevelopment and the policies required.[15] But few would deny that this new wave of research has taken economics in a different direction and has enriched our understanding of many aspects of developing societies.

Field experiments are fine-grained analyses focusing on specific communities, often one village at a time. The work on institutional development, by contrast, took both a much more macro view and a broad historical sweep. It focused on the institutions that made modern, prosperous capitalism possible: the rule of law, contract enforcement and property rights protection, political democracy. This research was inspired directly by work in other disciplines, on comparative political development and history. But the insights of those disciplines were refined and formulated into the kinds of models that economists are used to. In addition, much effort went into validating these ideas with sophisticated empirical analysis, using up-to-date statistical techniques.

The MIT economist Daron Acemoglu and the economics-trained Harvard political scientist James Robinson were the undisputed leaders of this new wave of work. Their first big research project that made a splash was a paper called "The Colonial Origins of Comparative Development," coauthored with their MIT colleague Simon Johnson.[16] The paper argued that patterns of institutions imposed by colonialists many centuries ago echo to this day. When colonialists settled in the new territories, they erected institutions that protected property rights and promoted growth and development. This was the case of the United States, Canada, Australia, and New Zealand primarily. When local health conditions did not permit settlement in large numbers, as in much of Africa, colonialists instead set up institutions that were more appropriate for the expropriation of resources, thereby delaying development. More than the argument itself, what made the paper inordinately successful was the imaginative empirical approach the authors used to validate their claim. In brief, they leveraged information on the mortality rates of early Western settlers (such as military officers and missionaries) to distinguish colonies by how hospitable the local environment was to erecting institutions that protect property rights.*

---

* The authors argued that early colonizers were more likely to set up good institutions in places where they encountered fewer mortality risks.

The paper was not without its critics. But it sparked a wave of new research on political economy, institutional development, and comparative economic history that harked back to an earlier era of social science inquiry when economics did not stand apart as a separate discipline. What were the deeper causes of capitalist development, beyond economic determinants such as saving and capital accumulation? Why did Spain and Portugal lag in development, after having led the world in the age of discoveries? What are the long-term economic implications of ethnic divisions, or of cultural attributes? These were old questions, even though the methods being used were new.[17] They were also "big" questions, attesting to the ability of the profession to successfully engage with some of the most significant issues in the social sciences.

These new areas of research may not have produced conclusive results, nor have they changed the face of economics forever. My point, rather, is that they have incorporated insights from other disciplines and have taken economics in novel directions. They suggest that the view of economics as an insular, inbred discipline closed to outside influences is more caricature than reality.

Moreover, the diseases that killed the Westerners were generally different from those that affected the native population. These assumptions allowed the authors to use settler mortality rates as an exogenous source of variation in the quality of institutions, independent of other determinants, such as proximity to trade routes, that may have affected long-term development paths.

Ambition and Modesty

Much of the criticism of economics boils down to the charge that economists are using the wrong model. They should be Keynesians, Marxians, or Minskyans instead of neoclassicals; demand-siders instead of supply-siders; behavioralists rather than rationalists; network theorists rather than methodological individualists; structuralists rather than interactionists. But simply switching to an alternative framework that itself lacks universality and captures only a particular slice of reality cannot be the solution. Insights of these alternative perspectives are, in fact, readily accommodated within standard modeling practices of economics, as I've argued. All these divides can be bridged by viewing economics as a collection of models, along with a system of navigation among models.

The discipline's most successful and celebrated practitioners exemplify this approach. The French economist Jean Tirole, who won the 2014 Nobel Prize in Economic Sciences for his work on regulation, is a good example. In typical fashion, he was deluged after his prize was announced by journalists seeking a quick take on the research that had brought him the recognition. But his interlocutors were in for some frustration. "There's no easy line in summarizing my contribution," he protested. "It is industry-specific. The way you regulate payment cards has nothing to do with the way that you regulate intellectual property or railroads. There are lots of idiosyncratic factors. That's what makes it all so interesting. It's very rich. . . . It's not a one-line thing."[18]

Economists who remain true to their discipline, like Tirole, are necessarily humble. Their discipline teaches them that on only very few matters can they express categorical views. Their responses to most questions necessarily take the form of "It depends," "I don't know," "Give me several years (and research funds) to study the problem," "There are three views on this . . . ," or perhaps, "Assume we have n goods and k consumers . . ." In this role they remain vulnerable to the criticism that they are ivory-tower academics, devoted to abstract mathematical models and fancy statistics, who fail to contribute to social understanding and the solution of public problems.

But as the science of trade-offs, economics deftly enlightens us on both sides of the ledger—the costs and benefits, the known and the unknown, the impossible and the feasible, the possible and the likely. Just as social reality admits a wide range of possibilities, economic models alert us to a variety of scenarios. Disagreements among economists are natural under the circumstances, and humility is the right attitude all around. It is better for the public to be exposed to these disagreements and uncertainties than to be lulled into a false sense of confidence about the answers that economics provides.

Humility would also make economists better citizens in the broader academic community of social science. Being up front about how much (or how little) they really know and understand would help them close some of the gap with other, nonpositiv-ist social science traditions. It might allow better dialogue with those who examine social reality through cultural, humanist, constructivist, or interpretive lenses. A core objection of the advocates of these alternative perspectives is that economics has a universalist, reductionist approach.[19] But with the multiplicity and context specificity of models at the front and center of eco-nomics, the differences become less serious than they first appear. For example, an economist's answer to the question "What about culture?" cannot and should not be "Culture is irrelevant." It should be "OK, let's try to write down a model of it"—meaning let's be clear about what we're assuming, what the causal chain is, and what the observable implications are. No sensible social scientist should turn his back on such a line of inquiry.

Economists still can aspire to greater ambition as public intellectuals or social reformers. They can be advocates of specific policies and institutions on many fronts—to improve the allocation of resources, unleash entrepreneurial energies, foster economic growth, and enhance equity and inclusion. They have much to contribute to the public debate in all these areas. Their exposure to diverse models of social life, capturing varieties of behavior and social outcomes, render them per-haps more alert to the possibilities of social progress than other social scientists are.* But they need to be aware that when they

---

* This is the "possibilism" that the great economist and social scientist Albert Hirschman advocated throughout his life. He rejected the

move into this role, they are inevitably stepping outside the well-defined scientific boundaries of their discipline. And they need to be explicit about this. Otherwise, they open themselves up to criticism that they are pushing beyond their expertise and passing off their own value judgments as science.

Economics provides many of the stepping-stones and analytic tools to address the big public issues of our time. What it doesn't provide is definitive, universal answers. Results taken from economics proper must be combined with values, judgments, and evaluations of an ethical, political, or practical nature. These last have very little to do with the discipline of economics, but everything to do with reality.

---

deterministic approaches, common to social sciences, that view outcomes as being rigidly pinned down by "structural" conditions, and instead argued for the power of ideas and small actions to have decisive effects. Philipp H. Lepenies, "Possibilism: An Approach to Problem-Solving Derived from the Life and Work of Albert O. Hirschman," *Development and Change* 39, no. 3 (May 2008): 437–59.

The Twenty Commandments

Ten Commandments for Economists

1. Economics is a collection of models; cherish their diversity.

2. It's a model, not *the* model.

3. Make your model simple enough to isolate specific causes and how they work, but not so simple that it leaves out key interactions among causes.

4. Unrealistic assumptions are OK; unrealistic *critical* assumptions are not OK.

5. The world is (almost) always second best.

6. To map a model to the real world you need explicit empirical diagnostics, which is more craft than science.

7. Do not confuse agreement among economists for certainty about how the world works.

8. It's OK to say "I don't know" when asked about the economy or policy.

9. Efficiency is not everything.

10. Substituting your values for the public's is an abuse of your expertise.

Ten Commandments for Noneconomists

1. Economics is a collection of models with no predetermined conclusions; reject any arguments otherwise.

2. Do not criticize an economist's model because of its assumptions; ask how the results would change if certain problematic assumptions were more realistic.

3. Analysis requires simplicity; beware of incoherence that passes itself off as complexity.

4. Do not let math scare you; economists use math not because they're smart, but because they're not smart enough.

5. When an economist makes a recommendation, ask what makes him/her sure the underlying model applies to the case at hand.

6. When an economist uses the term "economic welfare," ask what he/she means by it.

7. Beware that an economist may speak differently in public than in the seminar room.

8. Economists don't (all) worship markets, but they know better how they work than you do.

9. If you think all economists think alike, attend one of their seminars.

10. If you think economists are especially rude to noneconomists, attend one of their seminars.

NOTES

INTRODUCTION: The Use and Misuse of Economic Ideas

1. R. Preston McAfee and John McMillan, "Analyzing the Airwaves Auction," *Journal of Economic Perspectives* 10, no. 1 (Winter 1996): 159–75; Alvin E. Roth and Elliott Peranson, "The Redesign of the Matching Market for American Physicians: Some Engineering Aspects of Economic Design," *American Economic Review* 89, no. 4 (1999): 748–80; Louis Kaplow and Carl Shapiro, *Antitrust*, NBER Working Paper 12867 (Cambridge, MA: National Bureau of Economic Research, 2007); Ben Bernanke et al., *Inflation Targeting: Lessons from International Experience* (Princeton, NJ: Princeton University Press, 1999).

2. Steven D. Levitt and Stephen J. Dubner, *Freakonomics: A Rogue Economist Explores the Hidden Side of Everything* (New York: William Morrow, 2005).

CHAPTER 1: What Models Do

1. Ha-Joon Chang, *Economics: The User Guide* (London: Pelican Books, 2014), 3.

2. David Card and Alan Krueger, *Myth and Measurement: The New Economics of the Minimum Wage* (Princeton, NJ: Princeton University Press, 1997).

3. Dani Rodrik and Arvind Subramanian, "Why Did Financial Globalization Disappoint?" IMF Staff Papers 56, no. 1 (March 2009): 112–38.

4. Daniel Leigh et al., "Will It Hurt? Macroeconomic Effects of Fiscal Consolidation," in *World Economic Outlook* (Washington, DC: International Monetary Fund, 2010), 93–124, http://www.imf.org/external /pubs/ft/weo/2010/02/pdf/c3.pdf.

5. Ariel Rubinstein, "Dilemmas of an Economic Theorist," *Econometrica* 74, no. 4 (July 2006): 881.

6. Allan Gibbard and Hal R. Varian, "Economic Models," *Journal of Philosophy* 75, no. 11 (November 1978): 666.

7. Nancy Cartwright, "Models: Fables v. Parables," *Insights* (Durham Institute of Advanced Study) 1, no. 11 (2008).

8. The Colombia study I'm referring to is the well-known paper by Joshua Angrist, Eric Bettinger, and Michael Kremer: "Long-Term Educational Consequences of Secondary School Vouchers: Evidence from Administrative Records in Colombia," *American Economic Review* 96, no. 3 (2006): 847–62.

9. Nancy Cartwright and Jeremy Hardie, *Evidence-Based Policy: A Practical Guide to Doing It Better* (Oxford: Oxford University Press, 2012).

10. Milton Friedman, "The Methodology of Positive Economics," in *Essays in Positive Economics* (Chicago: University of Chicago Press, 1953).

11. Paul Pfleiderer, "Chameleons: The Misuse of Theoretical Models in Finance and Economics" (unpublished paper, Stanford University, 2014).

12. See Gibbard and Varian, "Economic Models," 671.

13. Nancy Cartwright, *Hunting Causes and Using Them: Approaches in Philosophy and Economics* (Cambridge: Cambridge University Press, 2007), 217.

14. Thomas C. Schelling, *The Strategy of Conflict* (Cambridge, MA: Harvard University Press, 1960); Schelling, Micromotives and Macrobehavior (New York: W. W. Norton, 1978).

15. Diego Gambetta, "'Claro!' An Essay on Discursive Machismo," in *Deliberative Democracy*, ed. Jon Elster (Cambridge: Cambridge University Press, 1998), 24.

16. Marialaura Pesce, "The Veto Mechanism in Atomic Differential Information Economies," *Journal of Mathematical Economics* 53 (2014): 33–45.

17. Jon Elster, *Explaining Social Behavior: More Nuts and Bolts for the Social Sciences* (Cambridge: Cambridge University Press, 2007), 461.

18. Golden Goose Award, "Of Geese and Game Theory: Auctions, Airwaves—and Applications," *Social Science Space*, July 17, 2014, http://www.socialsciencespace.com/2014/07/of-geese-and-game -theory-auctions-airwaves-and-applications.

19. Friedman, "Methodology of Positive Economics."

20. Alex Pertland, *Social Physics: How Good Ideas Spread—The Lessons from a New Science* (New York: Penguin, 2014), 11.

21. Duncan J. Watts, Everything Is Obvious: Once You Know the Answer (New York: Random House, 2011), Kindle edition, locations 2086–92.

22. Jorge Luis Borges, "On Exactitude in Science," in *Collected Fictions*, trans. Andrew Hurley (New York: Penguin, 1999).

23. Uskali Mäki, "Models and the Locus of Their Truth" *Synthese* 180 (2011): 47–63.

CHAPTER 2: The Science of Economic Modeling

1. John Maynard Keynes, *Essays in Persuasion* (New York: W. W. Norton, 1963), 358–73.

2. Adam Smith, *An Inquiry into the Nature and Causes of the Wealth of Nations*, 5th ed. (1789; repr., London: Methuen, 1904), I.ii.2.

3. The pencil example was based on an essay by Leonard E. Read called "I, Pencil: My Family Tree as Told to Leonard E. Read" (Irvington-on-Hudson, NY: Foundation for Economic Education, 1958), http://www.econlib.org/library/Essays/rdPncl1.html.

4. Kenneth J. Arrow, "An Extension of the Basic Theorems of Classical Welfare Economics," in *Proceedings of the Second Berkeley Symposium on Mathematical Statistics and Probability*, ed. J. Neyman (Berkeley: University of California Press, 1951), 507–32; Gerard Debreu, "The Coefficient of Resource Utilization," *Econometrica* 19 (July 1951): 273–92.

5. Paul Samuelson, "The Past and Future of International Trade Theory," in *New Directions in Trade Theory*, eds. A. Deardorff, J. Levinsohn, and R. M. Stern (Ann Arbor, MI: University of Michigan Press, 1995), 22.

6. David Ricardo, *On the Principles of Political Economy and Taxation* (London: John Murray, 1817), chap. 7.

7. Dani Rodrik, *The Globalization Paradox: Democracy and the Future of the World Economy* (New York: W. W. Norton, 2011), chap. 3.

8. David Ricardo, *On the Principles of Political Economy and Taxation*, 3rd ed. (London: John Murray, 1821), chap. 7, para. 7.17, http://www.econlib.org/library/Ricardo/ricP2a.html.

9. David Card, "The Impact of the Mariel Boatlift on the Miami Labor Market," *Industrial and Labor Relations Review* 43, no. 2 (January 1990): 245–57; George J. Borjas, "Immigration," in *The Concise Encyclopedia of Economics*, http://www.econlib.org/library/Enc1/Immigration.html, accessed December 31, 2014; Örn B. Bodvarsson, Hendrik F. Van den Berg, and Joshua J. Lewer, "Measuring Immigration's Effects on Labor Demand: A Reexamination of the Mariel Boatlift" (University of Nebraska—Lincoln, Economics Department Faculty Publications, August 2008).

10. James E. Meade, *The Theory of International Economic Policy*, vol. 2, *Trade and Welfare* (London: Oxford University Press, 1955); Richard G.

Lipsey and Kelvin Lancaster, "The General Theory of Second Best," *Review of Economic Studies* 24, no. 1 (1956–57): 11–32.

11. Avinash Dixit, "Governance Institutions and Economic Activity," *American Economic Review* 99, no. 1 (2009): 5–24.

12. Thomas C. Schelling, *The Strategy of Conflict* (Cambridge, MA: Harvard University Press, 1960); Schelling, *Micromotives and Macrobehavior* (New York: W. W. Norton, 1978).

13. For an excellent discussion with practical applications, see Avinash K. Dixit and Barry J. Nalebuff, *The Art of Strategy* (New York: W. W. Norton, 2008).

14. Joseph E. Stiglitz and Andrew Weiss, "Credit Rationing in Markets with Imperfect Information," *American Economic Review* 71, no. 3 (June 1981): 393–410.

15. Andrew Weiss, *Efficiency Wages: Models of Unemployment, Layoffs, and Wage Dispersion* (Princeton, NJ: Princeton University Press, 1990).

16. Itzhak Gilboa, Andrew Postlewaite, Larry Samuelson, and David Schmeidler, "Economic Models as Analogies" (unpublished paper, January 27, 2013), 6–7.

17. See, for example, my online debate for the *Economist* magazine with Harvard Business School professor Josh Lerner, July 12–17, 2010, http://www.economist.com/debate/debates/overview/177.

18. Carmen M. Reinhart and Kenneth S. Rogoff, *Growth in a Time of Debt,* NBER Working Paper 15639 (Cambridge, MA: National Bureau of Economic Research, 2010).

19. Thomas Herndon, Michael Ash, and Robert Pollin, "Does High Public Debt Consistently Stifle Economic Growth? A Critique of Reinhart and Rogoff" (Amherst: University of Massachusetts at Amherst, Political Economy Research Institute, April 15, 2013).

20. R. E. Peierls, "Wolfgang Ernst Pauli, 1900–1958," *Biographical Memoirs of Fellows of the Royal Society* 5 (February 1960): 186.

21. Albert Einstein, "Physics and Reality," in *Ideas and Opinions of Albert Einstein*, trans. Sonja Bargmann (New York: Crown, 1954), 290, cited in Susan Haack, "Science, Economics, 'Vision,'" *Social Research* 71, no. 2 (Summer 2004): 225.

CHAPTER 3: Navigating among Models

1. David Colander and Roland Kupers, *Complexity and the Art of Public Policy* (Princeton, NJ: Princeton University Press, 2014), 8.

2. Dani Rodrik, "Goodbye Washington Consensus, Hello Washington Confusion?: A Review of the World Bank's Economic Growth in the 1990s: Learning from a Decade of Reform," *Journal of Economic Literature* 44, no. 4 (December 2006): 973–87.

3. Ricardo Hausmann, Dani Rodrik, and Andres Velasco, "Growth Diagnostics," in *The Washington Consensus Reconsidered: Towards a New Global Governance*, eds. J. Stiglitz and N. Serra (New York: Oxford University Press, 2008).

4. The process is explained in greater detail, with examples from many countries, in Ricardo Hausmann, Bailey Klinger, and Rodrigo Wagner, *Doing Growth Diagnostics in Practice: A "Mindbook"*, CID Working Paper 177 (Cambridge, MA: Center for International Development at Harvard University, 2008).

5. Ricardo Hausmann, *Final Recommendations of the International Panel on ASGISA*, CID Working Paper 161 (Cambridge, MA: Center for International Development at Harvard University, 2008).

6. Ricardo Hausmann and Dani Rodrik, "Self-Discovery in a Development Strategy for El Salvador," *Economia: Journal of the Latin American and Caribbean Economic Association* 6, no. 1 (Fall 2005): 43–102.

7. Douglass C. North and Robert Paul Thomas, *The Rise of the Western World: A New Economic History* (Cambridge: Cambridge University Press, 1973).

8. Rochelle M. Edge and Refet S. Gürkaynak, *How Useful Are Estimated DSGE Model Forecasts?* Finance and Economics Discussion Series

(Washington, DC: Divisions of Research & Statistics and Monetary Affairs, Federal Reserve Board, 2011).

9. Barry Nalebuff, "The Hazards of Game Theory," *Haaretz*, May 17, 2006, http://www.haaretz.com/business/economy-finance/the-hazards-of -game-theory-1.187939. See also Avinash Dixit and Barry Nalebuff, *Thinking Strategically: The Competitive Edge in Business, Politics, and Everyday Life* (New York: W. W. Norton, 1993), chap 1.

10. Santiago Levy, *Progress against Poverty: Sustaining Mexico's Progresa-Oportunidades Program* (Washington, DC: Brookings Institution, 2006).

11. *Mexico—PROGRESA: Breaking the Cycle of Poverty* (Washington, DC: International Food Policy Research Institute, 2002), http://www .ifpri.org/sites/default/files/pubs/pubs/ib/ib6.pdf.

12. Edward Miguel and Michael Kremer, "Worms: Identifying Impacts on Education and Health in the Presence of Treatment Externalities," *Econometrica* 72, no. 1 (2004): 159–217.

13. Esther Duflo, Rema Hanna, and Stephen P. Ryan, "Incentives Work: Getting Teachers to Come to School," *American Economic Review* 102, no. 4 (June 2012): 1241–78.

14. David Roodman, "Latest Impact Research: Inching towards Generalization," Consultative Group to Assist the Poor (CGAP), April 11, 2012, http://www.cgap.org/blog/latest-impact-research-inching -towards-generalization.

15. Joshua D. Angrist, "Lifetime Earnings and the Vietnam Era Draft Lottery: Evidence from Social Security Administrative Records," *American Economic Review* 80, no. 3 (June 1990): 313–36.

16. Donald R. Davis and David E. Weinstein, "Bones, Bombs, and Break Points: The Geography of Economic Activity," *American Economic Review* 92, no. 5 (2002): 1269–89.

17. David R. Cameron, "The Expansion of the Public Economy: A Comparative Analysis," *American Political Science Review* 72, no. 4 (December 1978): 1243–61.

18. Dani Rodrik, "Why Do More Open Economies Have Bigger Governments?" *Journal of Political Economy* 106, no. 5 (October 1998): 997–1032.

19. Robert Sugden, "Credible Worlds, Capacities and Mechanisms" (unpublished paper, School of Economics, University of East Anglia, August 2008).

CHAPTER 4: Models and Theories

1. Andrew Gelman, "Causality and Statistical Learning," *American Journal of Sociology* 117 (2011): 955–66; Andrew Gelman and Guido Imbens, *Why Ask Why? Forward Causal Inference and Reverse Causal Questions*, NBER Working Paper 19614 (Cambridge, MA: National Bureau of Economic Research, 2013).

2. Dani Rodrik, "Democracies Pay Higher Wages," *Quarterly Journal of Economics* 114, no. 3 (August 1999): 707–38.

3. Thomas Piketty, Emmanuel Saez, and Stefanie Stantcheva, *Optimal Taxation of Top Labor Incomes: A Tale of Three Elasticities*, NBER Working Paper 17616 (Cambridge, MA: National Bureau of Economic Research, 2011).

4. J. R. Hicks, "Mr. Keynes and the 'Classics': A Suggested Interpretation," *Econometrica* 5, no. 2 (April 1937): 147–59.

5. John M. Keynes, "The General Theory of Employment," *Quarterly Journal of Economics* 51, no. 2 (February 1937): 209–23, cited by J. Bradford DeLong in "Mr. Hicks and 'Mr Keynes and the "Classics": A Suggested Interpretation': A Suggested Interpretation," June 20, 2010, http://delong.typepad.com/sdj/2010/06/mr-hicks-and-mr-keynes-and-the-classics-a-suggested-interpretation-a-suggested-interpretation.html.

6. Robert E. Lucas and Thomas Sargent, "After Keynesian Macroeconomics," *Federal Reserve Bank of Minneapolis Quarterly Review* 3, no. 2 (Spring 1979): 1–18.

7. John H. Cochrane, "Lucas and Sargent Revisited," *The Grumpy Economist* (blog), July 17, 2014, http://johnhcochrane.blogspot.jp/2014/07/lucas-and-sargent-revisited.html.

8. Robert E. Lucas Jr., "Macroeconomic Priorities," *American Economic Review* 93, no. 1 (March 2003): 1–14.

9. Robert E. Lucas, "Why a Second Look Matters" (presentation at the Council on Foreign Relations, New York, March 30, 2009), http://www.cfr.org/world/why-second-look-matters/p18996.

10. Holman W. Jenkins Jr., "Chicago Economics on Trial" (interview with Robert E. Lucas), *Wall Street Journal*, September 24, 2011, http://online.wsj.com/news/articles/SB10001424053111904194604576583382550849232.

11. Paul Krugman, "The Stimulus Tragedy," *New York Times*, February 20, 2014, http://www.nytimes.com/2014/02/21/opinion/krugman-the-stimulus-tragedy.html.

12. J. Bradford DeLong and Lawrence H. Summers, "Fiscal Policy in a Depressed Economy," *Brookings Papers on Economic Activity*, Spring 2012, 233–74.

13. Edward P. Lazear and James R. Spletzer, "The United States Labor Market: Status Quo or a New Normal?" (paper prepared for the Kansas City Fed Symposium, September 13, 2012).

14. Scott R. Baker, Nicholas Bloom, and Steven J. Davis, "Measuring Economic Policy Uncertainty" (unpublished paper, Stanford University, June 13, 2013); Daniel Shoag and Stan Veuger, "Uncertainty and the Geography of the Great Recession" (unpublished paper, John F. Kennedy School of Government, Harvard University, February 25, 2014).

15. The data are from the US Census Bureau; see "Income Gini Ratio for Households by Race of Householder, All Races," FRED Economic Data, Federal Reserve Bank of St. Louis, http://research.stlouisfed.org/fred2/series/GINIALLRH#, accessed July 24, 2014.

16. The World Top Incomes Database, http://topincomes.parisschoolofeconomics.eu/#Database, accessed July 24, 2014.

17. Edward E. Leamer, *Wage Effects of a U.S.–Mexican Free Trade Agreement*, NBER Working Paper 3991 (Cambridge, MA: National Bureau of Economic Research, 1992), 1.

18. Eli Berman, John Bound, and Zvi Griliches, "Changes in the Demand for Skilled Labor within US Manufacturing: Evidence from the Annual Survey of Manufacturers," *Quarterly Journal of Economics* 109, no. 2 (1994): 367–97.

19. Robert C. Feenstra and Gordon H. Hanson, "Foreign Direct Investment and Relative Wages: Evidence from Mexico's Maquiladoras," *Journal of International Economics* 42 (1997): 371–94.

20. Frank Levy and Richard J. Murnane, "U.S. Earnings and Earnings Inequality: A Review of Recent Trends and Proposed Explanations," *Journal of Economic Literature* 30 (September 1992): 1333–81; John Bound and George Johnson, "Changes in the Structure of Wages in the 1980s: An Evaluation of Alternative Explanations," *American Economic Review* 83 (June 1992): 371–92.

21. Lawrence Mishel, John Schmitt, and Heidi Shierholz, "Assessing the Job Polarization Explanation of Growing Wage Inequality," Economic Policy Institute, January 11, 2013, http://www.epi.org/publication/wp295-assessing-job-polarization-explanation-wage-inequality.

22. Albert O. Hirschman, "The Search for Paradigms as a Hindrance to Understanding," *World Politics* 22, no. 3 (April 1970): 329–43.

CHAPTER 5: When Economists Go Wrong

1. Thomas J. Sargent, "University of California at Berkeley Graduation Speech," May 16, 2007, https://files.nyu.edu/ts43/public/personal/UC_graduation.pdf.

2. Noah Smith, "Not a Summary of Economics," *Noahpinion* (blog), April 19, 2014, http://noahpinionblog.blogspot.com/2014/04/not-summary-of-economics.html; Paul Krugman, "No Time for Sargent," *New York Times* Opinion Pages, April 21, 2014, http://krugman.blogs.nytimes.com/2014/04/21/no-time-for-sargent/?module=BlogPost-Title&version=Blog%20Main&contentCollection=Opinion&action=Click&pgtype=Blogs&region=Body.

3. Greg Mankiw, "News Flash: Economists Agree," February 14, 2009, *Greg Mankiw's Blog,* http://gregmankiw.blogspot.com/2009/02/news -flash-economists-agree.html.

4. Richard A. Posner, "Economists on the Defensive—Robert Lucas," *Atlantic,* August 9, 2009, http://www.theatlantic.com/business/archive/2009/08/ economists-on-the-defensive-robert-lucas/22979.

5. Robert Shiller, *Irrational Exuberance,* 2nd ed. (Princeton, NJ: Princeton University Press, 2005).

6. Raghuram G. Rajan, "The Greenspan Era: Lessons for the Future" (remarks at a symposium sponsored by the Federal Reserve Bank of Kansas City, Jackson Hole, WY, August 27, 2005), https://www .imf.org/external/np/speeches/2005/082705.htm; Charles Ferguson, "Larry Summers and the Subversion of Economics," *Chronicle of Higher Education,* October 3, 2010, http://chronicle.com/article/ Larry-Summersthe/124790.

7. Eugene F. Fama, "Efficient Capital Markets: A Review of Theory and Empirical Work," *Journal of Finance* 25, no. 2 (May 1970): 383–417.

8. Edmund L. Andrews, "Greenspan Concedes Error on Regulation," *New York Times,* October 23, 2008, http://www.nytimes .com/2008/10/24/business/economy/24panel.html?_r=0.

9. John Williamson, "A Short History of the Washington Consensus" (paper commissioned by Fundación CIDOB for the conference "From the Washington Consensus towards a New Global Governance," Barcelona, September 24–25, 2004).

10. Dani Rodrik, "Goodbye Washington Consensus, Hello Washington Confusion?: A Review of the World Bank's *Economic Growth in the 1990s: Learning from a Decade of Reform,*" *Journal of Economic Literature* 44, no. 4 (December 2006): 973–87.

11. Dani Rodrik, "Getting Interventions Right: How South Korea and Taiwan Grew Rich," *Economic Policy* 10, no. 20 (1995): 53–107; Rodrik, "Second-Best Institutions," *American Economic Review* 98, no. 2 (May 2008): 100–104.

12. Stanley Fischer, "Capital Account Liberalization and the Role of the IMF," September 19, 1997, https://www.imf.org/external/np/speeches/1997/091997.htm#1.

13. "The Liberalization and Management of Capital Flows: An Institutional View," International Monetary Fund, November 14, 2012, http://www.imf.org/external/np/pp/eng/2012/111412.pdf.

14. Edward López and Wayne Leighton, *Madmen, Intellectuals, and Academic Scribblers: The Economic Engine of Political Change* (Stanford, CA: Stanford University Press, 2012).

15. Francisco Rodríguez and Dani Rodrik, "Trade Policy and Economic Growth: A Skeptic's Guide to the Cross-National Evidence," in *Macroeconomics Annual* 2000, eds. Ben Bernanke and Kenneth S. Rogoff (Cambridge, MA: MIT Press for NBER, 2001).

16. Mankiw, "News Flash: Economists Agree."

17. Mark R. Rosenzweig and Kenneth I. Wolpin, "Natural 'Natural Experiments' in Economics," *Journal of Economic Literature* 38, no. 4 (December 2000): 827–74.

18. Dani Rodrik, *The Globalization Paradox: Democracy and the Future of the World Economy* (New York: W. W. Norton, 2011), chap. 6. See also Rodrik, "In Praise of Foxy Scholars," Project Syndicate, March 10, 2014, http://www.project-syndicate.org/commentary/dani-rodrik-on-the-promise-and-peril-of-social-science-models.

CHAPTER 6: Economics and Its Critics

1. David Colander, Richard F. Holt, and J. Barkley Rosser, "The Changing Face of Mainstream Economics," *Review of Political Economy* 16, no. 4 (October 2004): 487.

2. For a good overview of the differences between economists' and anthropologists' perspectives, see Pranab Bardhan and Isha Ray, *Methodological Approaches in Economics and Anthropology*, Q-Squared Working Paper 17 (Toronto: Centre for International Studies, University of Toronto, 2006).

3. For a sampling of this work, see Samuel Bowles, "Endogenous Preferences: The Cultural Consequences of Markets and Other Economic
Institutions," *Journal of Economic Literature* 26 (1998): 75–111; George
A. Akerlof and Rachel E. Kranton *Identity Economics: How Our Identi-
ties Shape Our Work, Wages, and Well-Being* (Princeton, NJ: Princeton
University Press, 2010); Alberto Alesina and George-Marios Angele-
tos, "Fairness and Redistribution," *American Economic Review* 95, no.
4 (2005): 960–80; Alberto Alesina, Edward Glaeser, and Bruce Sacer-
dote, "Why Doesn't the United States Have a European-Style Welfare
State?" *Brookings Papers on Economic Activity*, no. 2 (2001): 187–254;
Raquel Fernandez, "Cultural Change as Learning: The Evolution of
Female Labor Force Participation over a Century," *American Economic
Review* 103, no. 1 (2013): 472–500; Roland Bénabou, Davide Ticchi,
and Andrea Vindigni, "Forbidden Fruits: The Political Economy of
Science, Religion, and Growth" (unpublished paper, Princeton Uni-
versity, December 2013).

4. Neil Gandal et al., "Personal Value Priorities of Economists," *Human
Relations* 58, no. 10 (October 2005): 1227–52; Bruno S. Frey and
Stephan Meier, "Selfish and Indoctrinated Economists?" *European
Journal of Law and Economics* 19 (2005): 165–71.

5. Michael J. Sandel, "What Isn't for Sale?" *Atlantic*, April 2012, http://
www.theatlantic.com/magazine/archive/2012/04/what-isnt-for-
sale/308902. See also Sandel, *What Money Can't Buy: The Moral Limits
of Markets* (New York: Farrar, Straus and Giroux, 2012).

6. Uri Gneezy and Aldo Rustichini, "A Fine Is a Price," *Journal of Legal
Studies* 29, no. 1 (January 2000): 1–17; Samuel Bowles, "Machiavelli's Mistake: Why Good Laws and No Substitute for Good Citizens"
(unpublished manuscript, 2014).

7. Sandel, "What Isn't for Sale?"

8. Albert O. Hirschman, *The Passions and the Interest: Political Arguments
for Capitalism before Its Triumph* (Princeton, NJ: Princeton University
Press, 1977); see also Hirschman, "Rival Interpretations of Market

Society: Civilizing, Destructive, or Feeble?" *Journal of Economic Literature* 20 (December 1982): 1463–84.

9. Dani Rodrik, "Occupy the Classroom," Project Syndicate, December 12, 2011, http://www.project-syndicate.org/commentary/occupy-the -classroom.

10. Simon Wren-Lewis, "When Economics Students Rebel," *Mainly Macro* (blog), April 24, 2014, http://mainlymacro.blogspot.co.uk-2014-04 -when=economocs=students=rebel.html.

11. Herbert A. Simon, "A Behavioral Model of Rational Choice," *Quarterly Journal of Economics* 69 (February 1955): 99–118; Richard R. Nelson and Sidney G. Winter, *An Evolutionary Theory of Economic Change* (Cambridge, MA: Belknap Press of Harvard University Press, 1982).

12. Daniel Kahneman, Paul Slovic, and Amos Tversky, *Judgement under Uncertainty: Heuristics and Biases* (Cambridge: Cambridge University Press, 1982).

13. Werner F. M. De Bondt and Richard Thaler, "Does the Stock Market Overreact?" *Journal of Finance* 40, no. 3 (1985): 793–805.

14. David Laibson, "Golden Eggs and Hyperbolic Discounting," Quarterly Journal of Economics 112, no. 2 (1997): 443–77; Brigitte C. Madrian and Dennis F. Shea, "The Power of Suggestion: Inertia in 401(k) Participation and Savings Behavior," *Quarterly Journal of Economics* 116, no. 4 (2000): 1149–87; Jeffrey Liebman and Richard Zeckhauser, *Simple Humans, Complex Insurance, Subtle Subsidies*, NBER Working Paper 14330 (Cambridge, MA: National Bureau of Economic Research, 2008); Esther Duflo, Michael Kremer, and Jonathan Robinson, *Nudging Farmers to Use Fertilizer: Theory and Experimental Evidence from Kenya*, NBER Working Paper 15131 (Cambridge, MA: National Bureau of Economic Research, 2009).

15. See, for example, Angus Deaton, "Instruments of Development: Randomization in the Tropics, and the Search for the Elusive Keys to Economic Development" (Research Program in Development Studies, Center for Health and Wellbeing, Princeton University, January 2009).

16. Daron Acemoglu, Simon Johnson, and James A. Robinson, "The Colonial Origins of Comparative Development: An Empirical Investigation," *American Economic Review* 91, no. 5 (December 2001): 1369–1401.

17. A good overall synthesis of this work can be found in Daron Acemoglu and James Robinson, *Why Nations Fail: The Origins of Power, Prosperity, and Poverty* (New York: Crown, 2012).

18. Binyamin Appelbaum, "Q. and A. with Jean Tirole, Economics Nobel Winner," *New York Times*, October 14, 2014 (http://www.nytimes .com/2014/10/15/upshot/q-and-a-with-jean-tirole-nobel-prize-win- ner.html?_r=0&abt=0002&abg=0).

19. See, for example, the essays in Paul Rabinow and William M. Sulli- van, eds., *Interpretive Social Science: A Second Look* (Berkeley: University of California Press, 1987).

INDEX

Page numbers in *italics* refer to illustrations.